Families, Crime
and Juvenile Justice

Joseph L. DeVitis & Linda Irwin-DeVitis
General Editors

Vol. 10

PETER LANG
New York • Washington, D.C./Baltimore • Bern
Frankfurt am Main • Berlin • Brussels • Vienna • Oxford

Richard Hil &
Anthony McMahon

Families, Crime and Juvenile Justice

PETER LANG
New York • Washington, D.C./Baltimore • Bern
Frankfurt am Main • Berlin • Brussels • Vienna • Oxford

Library of Congress Cataloging-in-Publication Data
Hil, Richard.
Families, crime and juvenile justice / by Richard Hil and Anthony McMahon.
p. cm. — (Adolescent cultures, school & society; vol. 10)
Includes bibliographical references and index.
1. Juvenile delinquents—Family relationships. 2. Juvenile delinquency—
Prevention. 3. Juvenile justice, Administration of—Social aspects.
4. Social control. I. McMahon, Anthony. II. Title. III. Series.
HV9069 .H58   364.36—dc21   99-054868
ISBN 0-8204-4057-4
ISSN 1091-1464

Die Deutsche Bibliothek-CIP-Einheitsaufnahme
Hil, Richard:
Families, crime and juvenile justice / Richard Hil and Anthony McMahon.
—New York; Washington, D.C./Baltimore; Bern;
Frankfurt am Main; Berlin; Brussels; Vienna; Oxford: Lang.
(Adolescent cultures, school & society; Vol. 10)
ISBN 0-8204-4057-4

Cover design by Joni Holst

The paper in this book meets the guidelines for permanence and durability
of the Committee on Production Guidelines for Book Longevity
of the Council of Library Resources.

© 2001 Peter Lang Publishing, Inc., New York

All rights reserved.
Reprint or reproduction, even partially, in all forms such as microfilm,
xerography, microfiche, microcard, and offset strictly prohibited.

Printed in the United States of America

ACKNOWLEDGMENTS

There are many people we wish to thank for their support in this project. First and foremost, we wish to thank the twenty families who spoke to us of their experiences of juvenile offending. We thank Alan Carter, Ross Butterfield, and Ron Unwin of the Queensland Department of Families, Youth, and Community Care for assisting us in meeting the families. We thank our research assistants, Amma Buckley, Selina Hale, and Cathy Illin, who assisted in the task of interviewing, and Jeannette Cole for transcribing the interviews. We also thank Brenda Bendall and Joanne Baker for their editorial asistance. Finally, we acknowledge the assistance of James Cook University for giving us two Merit Research Grants to undertake the project.

Contents

1.	Listening to Parents	1
2.	Families and Juvenile Crime	15
3.	Families and Juvenile Justice	27
4.	Researching Families of Juvenile Offenders	45
5.	The Watts Family: A Case Study	65
6.	Parents' Experiences of Juvenile Offending	83
7.	Finding Fault: Families' Explanations for Offending Behaviour	107
8.	Parents and the Police, Family Services and the Court	131
9.	Making Parents Pay: Parental Restitution	155
10.	Learning Some Lessons	173
	Conclusion	187
	References	191
	Index	201

CHAPTER ONE

Listening to Parents

> What is absent [in the homes of offending children] is the persistent exercise by parents of moral control over their children. Without constant surveillance and moral control over children, there is always the possibility that they will slide into crime (Judge Fred Maguire, President of the Queensland Children's Court 1995: 122).

Over recent years there has been no shortage of speculation about the causes of juvenile crime. Feminism, working mothers, secularism, permissiveness, television, unemployment, poverty, disadvantage, boredom, and disaffection have all been blamed for the apparent slide into lawlessness. Particular attention, however, has been focused on the family. Crime has been attributed by politicians, shock-jocks, and social commentators to family breakup/breakdown, lack of parental control, responsibility, and discipline. Governments in America, Australia, and Britain have introduced tough new laws to punish the neglectful parents of offending children, and the family has been co-opted ever more deeply into the culture of crime control (Hil 1998).

The links drawn between juvenile crime and family life are hardly new. They have been the subject of extensive empirical inquiry over many years. Researchers from a variety of disciplines (criminology, sociology, psychology, geography, and so forth) have employed an assortment of methodological techniques aimed at establishing whether the structure, type, and dynamics of family life have any bearing upon the emergence of crime and delinquency.

While such investigations have often been prolonged and rigorous, as well as highly influential in social policy terms, they have yielded very limited conclusions. Indeed, most of the studies in this area have generally failed to further our understanding of the complex interrelationship between the private domain of the family and the overarching social, economic, and political forces that have powerful effects on this social institution (Holman 1995; Wells and Rankin 1986; Utting 1994). Moreover, attempts by researchers to conceptualize the relationship between the family and crime and delinquency have tended to locate their analyses firmly on the terrain of pathology and parental failure. Typically in such studies, issues of poverty, racism, unemployment, low income, and so forth, are relegated to background or environmental influences.

In this book we argue that much of the empirical research dealing with families and crime is both analytically and conceptually flawed. The resulting discourse is often based on the erroneous assumption that the families of those labeled as juvenile offenders or young offenders are demonstrably different from other law-abiding households—more argumentative, conflictual, discordant, and less close, loving, caring, and responsible. This characterization of particular types of families assumes that it is possible to identify a cohort of those kinds of people who stand apart from the rest of us (Roach-Anleu 1991: 9; see also Young 1996). It follows, therefore (or so the argument goes), that if the family is indeed the main generator of deviant behaviours, and if parents cannot contain the behaviours of their errant children, then ameliorative action may be required. Given the dominance of psychological research in this area, it comes as no surprise that the assumptions of inherent dysfunction and criminogenic tendency have fed directly into the intervention strategies of social workers, psychologists, community workers, youth workers and family therapists (Carrington 1993; Rose 1990; Simpson 1991; Utting, Bright, and Henricson 1994).

While it must be acknowledged that the dynamics of family life do, of course, have some bearing on the creation of crime and delinquency, it is misleading to focus solely on families, or particular types of families. To do so is not only to ignore the sociopolitical contexts of offending but also to deny the differential ways in which crime control is administered (Hogg and Brown 1998). In examining crime in relation to families, and particularly those families that experience the most intense forms of policing, it is necessary to develop a critical social theory that takes us beyond simplistic assumptions of the bad, dysfunctional or problem family (Cook 1997).

Such a theory is necessarily cognizant of the way individualistic assumptions have colonized studies of families and crime. One result of this has been the almost total disregard of what family members themselves have to say about offending and its consequences. Indeed, it is striking to note that despite the steady flow of empirical studies over the past few decades, little or nothing is known about the ways in which criminalized young people and their families describe and interpret their lived experiences. The subjects of empirical research are thus rendered conspicuous by their silence. The personal narratives of family members, their stories, accounts, and experiences are regarded as secondary to the interpretative extrapolations of social scientists, thereby reinforcing the positivistic separation between expert and subject (Foucault 1977; Hall 1995).

In contrast, we maintain that the valorization of the subject's voice, of personal narrative and experience, is essential not only in contesting the often spurious assumptions of many empirical studies, but also in enabling those caught up in systems of control to voice their experiences in their own terms. While such narratives have limitations, they nonetheless offer an invaluable insight into the means by which the subjects of control systems articulate their experiences. Indeed, it is in the telling of personal stories that we begin to appreciate the importance of the meanings that individuals in families attach to their situations. Much is to be gained therefore from listening to the ways in which family members talk about their interactions with agencies of social control (Cohen 1985).

At the same time, however, it is necessary to locate the articulations of subjects in the context of prevailing social, economic, and political conditions (Connell and Irving 1992: 4–5). Only in this way can we begin to make sense of some of the complex interactions that occur within the family household. This suggests the need to locate empirical inquiry in a theoretical framework that is sensitive to the historical and wider socio-political and economic conditions that influence the daily lives of family members. Broadly speaking, the fact that criminalized offenders and their families are generally drawn from the most disadvantaged and underprivileged backgrounds suggests the need to address the issue of offending in its wider contexts (Hudson 1993, Youth Justice Coalition 1990: 27).

Locating the research

Townsville is a large coastal city in the north-east of the Australian state of Queensland. About 120,000 people live in this city in the dry tropics and in its nearby twin city, Thuringowa. Like many rural cities, juvenile crime, its prevention and control, are important topics in the local press. This research has been conducted amidst the steady reporting in North Queensland newspapers of crimes committed by juveniles. The talk in Townsville, as elsewhere, is of teen gangs, crime waves, epidemics of offending, and the need for tough solutions and the restoration of law and order.

The supposed role of parents in juvenile crime also received attention in local newspapers. Reports focused on the alleged failure of parents to curb the anti-social activities of their children and, as if in response, a Townsville Children's Court Magistrate was reported as requiring three parents to appear in court to argue why they should not pay for the crimes committed by their children (*Townsville Bulletin*, May 30, 1996). The (then) State Attorney General flagged changes to the *Juvenile Justice Act* of 1992 and commented that this important legislation will shift home responsibility to both the offenders and their parents. The community has had enough (*Townsville Bulletin*, May 30, 1996).

What were these crimes? Most juvenile crimes reported in the papers involved stealing (including shoplifting and car theft) and breaking and entering into houses. The *Townsville Bulletin* (June 18, 1996) reported that there were 290 break-ins by juveniles in April 1996 and 327 in May. There were few crimes of violence. In answer to a reporter's query whether police 'were quite capable of dealing with the city's crime wave,' police reported that 'car thefts involving joy-riding teenagers had dropped and few random bashings of schoolboys had been reported' (*Townsville Bulletin*, April 25, 1996).

> The crimes juveniles actually commit, however, are almost irrelevant to the debate about juvenile offending. Juvenile offending, at least in the Townsville print media, has become a springboard for political aspirants and a soapbox for vigilantes with solutions that hark back to the supposed good old days when juveniles and indigenous peoples were kept quiet and out of sight. Certainly, the collectivization of all young people into criminal gangs with headlines such as 'Teen gang terror in West End' (*Townsville Sun* April 3, 1996) and 'Teen gang's theft brazen' (*Independent News* May 15, 1996) serves to create an atmosphere of fear, anxiety and paranoia about young people in groups. As the Townsville Victim of Crime Association secretary said, '90 per cent of juveniles not involved in criminal activities were now being victimized by the wider community, particularly groups of students seen as 'gangs' (*Townsville Bulletin* May 31, 1996). Young people are seen as lawless, violent and uncontrolled and, thereby, a source of incredible frustration to many members of the Townsville/Thuringowa communities. (McMahon 1997: 76)

Community frustration is further exacerbated by the perception, fueled by local newspapers, that juveniles do not receive appropriate punishment for their crimes. 'The ideas that juvenile offenders are rarely caught, that police are not that concerned about catching them, that even if they are apprehended courts give lenient sentences so that they return to torment people again, is accepted wisdom in the local print media' (McMahon 1997: 77). When convicted juveniles are sent to jail, even incarceration is seen as a soft option: 'The city's diehard juvenile criminals are sent to the Cleveland Correctional Centre where they are treated like kings, according to two workers at the centre. Once they did make it to Cleveland, instead of being punished for their crimes, they enjoyed privileges law-abiding youths would not receive in their own homes, they said' (*Townsville Sun* April 17, 1996).

A further aspect of this research is the Indigenous background of many of the juvenile offenders. There are two Indigenous peoples in Australia, the Aborigines, who live mainly on the continental mainland or on the island of Tasmania, and the Torres

Strait Islanders, who originally came from the islands of the Torres Strait between the top of the state of Queensland and the neighbouring country of Papua New Guinea. Many Torres Strait islanders now live on the mainland, especially in North Queensland. Indigenous Australians suffer severe social, political, economic, and personal hardship, much of it the result of the occupation of their countries over the last 200 years and the extermination and assimilation policies that flowed from European invasion and settlement. Indigenous Australians are two percent of the Australian population, ten percent of the population of the Townsville region and 58 percent of the juvenile offenders in the Townsville region. Race, therefore, is a crucial subtext to any discussion of juvenile offending in North Queensland (McMahon 1997).

Researching families' stories

Traditionally, studies of families with juvenile offenders have tended to focus on atomized features of family life. This research, in contrast, has been guided by Denzin's interpretive interactionist approach which 'attempts to make the world of lived experience directly accessible to the reader. Such an approach endeavours to capture the voices, emotions, and actions of those studied' (Denzin 1989: 10). The research is an example of what Knapp (1995) calls qualitative description to illuminate the meaning social arrangements have for participants and of bottom-up research that focuses on the consumer and consumption of services.

Gaining entry to do research requires negotiation with multiple formal and informal gatekeepers (Lincoln and Guba 1985). Contact was first made with administrative staff in the Queensland Department of Families, Youth, and Community Care (DFYCC) in the regional city of Townsville in order to obtain support and cooperation for the project. This department, known colloquially as Family Services, has responsibility for the policing and care of juvenile offenders within the State of Queensland. Managers and family care workers were enthusiastic about the research and agreed to support our proposal. Approval for the research from the Department's Head Office in the state capital, Brisbane, took over six months and during this time no field research was undertaken. After gaining approval, we sought and obtained ethics approval from James Cook University for the research.

Only at this stage did we approach DFYCC staff working in the area of juvenile justice to help identify and make contact with parents of children who were repeat offenders. We emphasized that we were interested in interviewing family members about their experiences of the day-to-day concerns and issues generated by the behaviour of young offenders. We took pains to emphasize that the research was not an evaluation of their work or of the families but an attempt to hear, in the parents' own words, how families live with juvenile offenders. We told the workers that we were seeking parents to interview who had child(ren) with a history of petty offending, who were willing to tell of their experiences, and who lived locally. It was also important to interview families who reflected the general population of juvenile offenders. Thus, among the families we sought were single-parent families, two-parent families, and Indigenous families.

The DFYCC staff then identified suitable families and approached them to obtain their agreement to participate in the study. Seventeen families were initially identified in this way and three more families were added later to the sample when the research was widened slightly to consider the issue of parental restitution. This method, while appearing cumbersome because of the layers of negotiation between the parents and the researchers, ensured that the parents who did speak to us were willing to do so.

Finally, once each family had agreed to take part, one of the researchers conducted a preliminary interview, either by phone or in person, to outline the research and ensure that they were fully informed of the nature and purpose of the project. This was the first time the parents met the researchers, and it was only then that the formal interviewing began. At all steps in the process of gaining access and permission from the parents to proceed, we were conscious that the research process and the subject matter required a sensitive approach to families whose reception might range from cooperation or indifference to unease and hostility (Lee and Renzetti 1993). In fact, though parents were most willing to tell their stories, some offenders also consented to be interviewed, as did other family members.

Interviewing and interpretation

The data for this study were derived from a series of in-depth semi-structured interviews (Minichiello, Aroni, Timewell, and Alexander 1990) with parents and family members with children regarded as repeat petty offenders. Since the purpose of the research was to understand how families, and especially parents, coped with children who were offenders, the interview questions focused on four main areas of interest to the researchers. First, who was in the family household and how had the child's offending changed the dynamics of family living? Second, what were the parents' reactions on first becoming aware of their children's offending and what were their reactions to their children's continued offending? Third, how would the parents assess their relationships with the police, DFYCC officers and staff of other juvenile justice agencies, and the officials of the Children's Court? Fourth, what would parents say to politicians and media commentators who blamed parents for their children's offending?

The number of interviews with families varied. In some interviews, all aspects of the interview schedule were covered in one visit. With other families, two and sometimes more interviews were conducted in order to cover the questions on the interview schedule. There were five different interviewers for the 20 families including an Indigenous interviewer for most of the Aboriginal families. All interviews were audiotaped and transcribed in full. During the course of the research, the two principal researchers met regularly and noted conversations, observations, and emerging themes. This debriefing included exploring methodological decisions and future plans, critiquing the research process, maintaining perspective in the research and reading drafts of the research.

At the completion of the period of interviewing, the transcribed interviews were coded manually into 95 categories and subcategories. These categories were subsumed into four major themes, and these themes have become the basis of chapters in this book. In writing the chapters, we have been guided by a descriptive realist style that attempts to allow those being interpreted to speak for themselves (Denzin 1989). Descriptive realism reveals the conflictual, contradictory nature of lived experience and realizes that no single interpretation can completely capture problematic events.

The families in the study

Twenty families were interviewed for this study. Most parents interviewed were the mothers of the offenders. Seven families were of Aboriginal descent (Butcher, Ralph, O'Connor, Heatley, Joyce, Perkins, and Ryan families), and eight (six males and two females) of the offending children were Aboriginal; none were from Torres Strait Islander families. Three families were immigrants to Australia: the Jones and Smith families from the United Kingdom and the Marcos family from the Philippines. Offending children in the families comprised six females and 17 males. Their ages ranged from eleven years to 17 years. All names have been anonymized to safeguard the identities of the families and the offending children.

Interestingly, most families had only one child who had been or was offending during the course of the research. The families described themselves as 'no frills,' 'normal' or 'similar to their relatives and friends.' For many participants, the concept of family extended beyond the immediate family of partners, children, and siblings and included parents, grandparents (who figured prominently in extended family relationships), aunts, uncles, brothers, and sisters. Jody Fraser, for example, who resides near her mother, maintained regular contact with her: 'I drop in a few times a day to see my mother and my brother comes over regularly.' Chris Watts, too, described his wife Susan's regular interaction with her family by saying, 'She phones her mother once a day and they see each other a few times a week as well.' Overall, the participants described their family lives as 'normal' and most participants valued and made sure they maintained high levels of family and extended family interactions.

Table 1. The families and their offending children

	Families	Offending Children/Age	Interviewees
1.	McLure	Cain (17)	mother
2.	Smith	Peter (17)	mother
3.	Jones	Tim (17)	mother
4.	Towner	Brendan (15)	mother, father, sister, offender
5.	Santorini	Paul (17)	stepmother, father
6.	Butcher*	Tom (16)	mother
7.	Ralph*	Helen (14)	mother
8.	O'Connor*	John (11)	grandmother
9.	Carter	Mary (14)	mother, father, offender
10.	Mackey	Matthew (12)	mother, stepfather
11.	Heatley*	Sam (17) Nicholas (16)	mother
12.	Fraser	James (16)	mother, offender
13.	Joyce*	Amy (13)	mother, father, DFYCC worker
14.	Watts	John (16)	mother, stepfather, grandmother, offender
15.	Perkins*	Robert (15)	mother, offender
16.	Reynolds	Lester (12)	mother
17.	Fleming	Natalie (17)	mother
18.	Webb	Carl (17) Jane (16)	mother
19.	Marcos	Richard (17) Tess (16)	mother
20.	Ryan*	Luke (15)	mother, father

(Names with an asterisk (*) indicate the family is of Aboriginal descent)

Strengths and limitations of the study

Inevitably, during the course of this research, parents talked about various aspects of their lives. Not surprisingly, the intricacies of family life were often revealed in such accounts. Occasionally, we also obtained a glimpse into some of the material aspects of people's lives and the impact of this on the offending behaviours of young people. For some families, material considerations appeared more important than for others. We were able to conclude from this that, despite our own insistence that attention should be drawn to the material realities of people's lives, the families caught up in systems of crime control preferred to give emphasis to intrafamily relationships rather than to factors of poverty and lack of employment. What we do know about juvenile offenders who end up in the criminal justice system is that they tend to come from poor and disadvantaged backgrounds. Studies still need to be conducted on the way in which particular material constraints are having an increasing impact on the lives of those living in the most disadvantaged (and usually over-policed) communities. Such research becomes even more pressing when we consider the growing levels of poverty in Australia and other developed countries and the drive towards more intense and tough forms of crime control.

No single study can claim to do justice to the complexities associated with juvenile crime or to the family reactions to it. The diverse and unique nature of family life mitigates against any sweeping generalizations in this area of study. Moreover, the differences in ages of those classified as juvenile, the social and cultural backgrounds of the young people and their families, and the diversity of family composition merely add to the complexity of analysis. In short, the study has a number of strengths and weaknesses. Its primary strength is that it at least provides the beginnings of a more qualitative approach to the study of family reactions to juvenile offending. The data reveal the complex and diverse nature of these reactions which often belie the more conventional findings of empirical studies in this area. It is our hope that this study lays the foundations for further research on juvenile crime and families.

Plan of the book

Chapter Two focuses on the growing emphasis given to the family over recent years. We argue that concerns over the decline of the family and the shift away from traditional values has, in part, set the context for the emergence of family based crime control initiatives. In Chapter Three, we consider a range of developments in western systems of justice that have led increasingly to the co-option of the family into localized approaches to crime control. It is argued that the emergence of community control—an alliance of active citizens and state sponsored control agencies—has led to the increasing absorption of the family, school, and neighbourhood into the apparatus of crime control. We further argue, however, that the inclusion of the community in the struggle against crime is ensured through a number of disciplinary measures designed to engage the active compliance of parents in the care and control of their children. Such measures have been legitimated by the state under the individualistic pretext of increasing personal and family responsibility. Chapter Four reviews the literature on families and crime. We maintain that the results stemming from this literature are narrow and inconclusive. In pursuing predictive indicators, empirical researchers have glossed over the personal experiences of the research subjects.

Chapter Five is the story of one family's experiences of an offending child and their response to his offending and to the police and social workers involved. Chapter Six draws extensively on participants' accounts of the juvenile justice system, recording the parents' reactions to the news of their children's offending, and the consequent aftershocks for families. Their stories contradict the prevalent belief that the parents of juvenile offenders are indifferent to the offending of their children. Chapter Seven provides parents' and offenders' explanations of the causes of offending and gives parents' reactions to the idea that they are to blame for their children's offending. Chapter Eight reports on the ways family members experience the intervention of state officials and the impact this has had on the ability of parents to prevent further offending. Parents comment on alternative ways in which they could have dealt with their son or daughter's offending and on the support offered by state officials.

In Chapter Nine, we report on interviews with a subset of four families who were ordered by the courts (in Queensland, Australia) to show cause why they should not pay restitution for their children's crimes. Finally, in Chapter Ten, we argue that current practices of institutionalized regulation and surveillance provide little benefit to families faced with the problem of juvenile offending. We contend that intervention from an organizational perspective needs to be informed by an understanding of the problems that beset many families and the efforts they have already made to deal with the offending of their children. At a minimum this will require workers to develop skills that address not only the material circumstances of families but also the concrete, lived experiences of family members.

CHAPTER TWO

Families and Juvenile Crime

'Penalties should be imposed on parents of kids who break the law. Parents must take responsibility for the actions of their children.' (Peter Lindsay, Federal Member for Herbert in the Australian Parliament. Press release, Townsville, April 23, 1996)

'A further criticism of recent debates about the family would be its tendency to concentrate on personal responsibilities, to the exclusion of other pressures which make it difficult to be a "good enough" parent' (Utting 1995: 12).

'Responsibility is so synonymous with the family that it almost qualifies as an alternative spelling' (Hill 1994).

This book has been researched and written against the background of a protracted moral panic over juvenile crime. Public discourse in western countries has been dominated in recent times by references to juvenile crime waves, spiraling crime rates, epidemics of offending, lawlessness, teen gangs and so forth. There have also been numerous and persistent calls for tough government action (Davis 1996: 232–254; Hogg and Brown 1998: 38).

The part played by parents in creating the so-called juvenile crime problem has also received considerable media attention over recent years. In addition to the emphasis on offending, reports have focused on the apparent failure of parents to curb the antisocial behaviours of their children. Parents have been blamed directly for failing to exercise enough control and supervision over their errant children, or accused of lacking the necessary parenting skills to bring up law-abiding and well adjusted children. Traces of this parent-blaming discourse are found regularly in the columns of newspapers.

This emphasis on parental failure has also been used more broadly as an explanation for the supposed rise in juvenile crime, as well as a pretext for the introduction of various hard-line judicial penalties. As already suggested, parents have been blamed on two major grounds: first, for being negligent in their duties of care and supervision and second, for lacking the necessary skills to bring up law-abiding children. These assertions tend to go hand-in-hand and are applied most often in relation to problem or dysfunctional families (Cook 1997). Such families, it is said, reflect a general decline in moral standards brought about by a collapse of the traditional family and traditional family values. As we will show, public talk about the lack of parental responsibility is overlaid with discourses that represent current family problems as reflective of various ideologies and social movements that arose during earlier decades. We further suggest that the moral dimension evident in much public discourse on juvenile crime is closely connected to a range of overarching governmental approaches that seek to explain economic downturn by placing the blame for crime and other social problems on the shoulders of feckless and irresponsible people. Crime is thus seen as symptomatic of the decline of the moral order, and is most closely related to family breakdown and widespread parental negligence.

Focus on the family

As suggested above, the condition of the modern family has become one of the major concerns of politicians, media spokespersons, and academics (Sarantakos 1996). Indeed, the well-being of this institution is often seen as linked inextricably to the stability of society itself (Gilding 1997). Any change to the family is therefore viewed with considerable interest and/or trepidation (Gittins 1993). According to some commentators, the changing composition of the modern family merely reflects the particular cultural norms and social values of any given society, while for others such changes signal a crisis in the moral order and of apocalyptic times ahead. There is talk in some circles of family breakdown and growing social disintegration while others bemoan the passing of a mythical golden age in which everyone knew their rightful place. Such nostalgia is often accompanied by calls for a return of the traditional family made up of mum, dad, and two kids (Richards 1990).

Over recent years changes in family formations have invoked considerable unease among the major political parties of most western liberal states. Indeed, the issue of the family has come to occupy the center ground of social policy discourse in Britain, the United States, and Australia where governments have attempted to develop a range of policies aimed at addressing many of the concerns relating to this institution. Some of these policies have been directed towards supporting families through concessionary fiscal measures and the provision of various support services, whereas other policies have been concerned with lessening the perceived reliance of the family upon the state. In the wake of the International Year of the Family in 1994, many governments have sought to elevate the family to the top of the social-policy agenda. In common with governments in the United States and Britain, the coalition government in Australia has portrayed itself as the guardian of the family. Such has been the intensity of discussion on this matter over recent years that the leading Australian national newspaper referred to the family as the 'Issue of the Nineties' (*The Australian*, May 16, 1994).

Although public deliberations on the state of the family are hardly new (Finch 1994), recent anxieties have been generated by a number of factors. Some of these anxieties relate to a growing public awareness of the social and economic divisions in western societies, and the particular consequences of these for poor and disadvantaged families (Briggs 1994), and a growing sense of disenchantment among the ranks of middle-class families who point to a fall in their general standards of living. The dominant concern over the family, however, relates to its apparent fracturing into an array of broken, incomplete, and dysfunctional units (Weeks and Wilson 1993). The high divorce rate and the increase of sole-parent households are repeatedly cited as indicators of the breakdown or new decline of the traditional family (Pinkney 1994). According to the advocates of tradition, the current disintegration of the family has been accompanied by a host of negative consequences, including the erosion of parental discipline, discord, child abuse and neglect, teenage alcoholism, drug (ab)use, youth suicide, and crime and delinquency. Although the evidence suggests that such behaviours are less prevalent among most young people than is often thought (Australian Law Reform Commission 1997; White and Wynn 1997), their origins are nonetheless said to be found in the increasingly fragmented state of the modern family.

Political discourse: The seeds of destruction

The declining fortunes of the family tend to be explained in a variety of ways. Advocates of the profamily movement and the Christian New Right in Britain and the United States attribute the current state of the family to a number of fundamental changes in the moral climate over the past few decades. During the 1980s various New Right intellectuals and government leaders, most notably Margaret Thatcher and Ronald Reagan, linked the decline of the family to increasing social disorder. Abbott and Wallace describe the New Right's views on the family as follows:

> Central to the moral decay of society is a breakdown in family life and in the family taking on responsibility for the economic support of its members and for their morality. The breakdown of the family—as evidenced by working mothers (who by taking part time work fail to put the needs of their children first), increased divorce rates, higher numbers of single parent families and open homosexuality—is also blamed for increased crime rates, high unemployment and drug taking. Society's social problems are seen as the result of the breakdown of family life. (Abbott and Wallace 1992: 9)

The ailing state of the family was therefore seen by the New Right as the harbinger of all manner of antisocial behaviours. The shift away from the nuclear family (the family of tradition), in which roles and responsibilities of family members were marked out along patriarchal lines, was seen as signaling the decline of the family, and therefore of society itself. New Right intellectuals attributed this decline to liberal ideologies and social movements that flourished from the 1960s onwards. Feminism, permissiveness, secularism, and socialism were blamed for fostering a set of ideas that undermined the traditional structures of moral authority. Underpinning such criticism was a deep nostalgia for a time when the family, with all its constituent members in place (father at work, mother at home with the children), could lay claim to be the solid foundation of a cohesive society. As Abbott and Wallace (1992: 6) point out: 'The appeal of the New Right is one of nostalgia—for a lost past when children respected their parents, the crime rate was low, marriages were for life and the streets were safe for everyone to walk in. What is concealed . . . is that [this image] was never a reality but an ideal, a middle class dream.'

The twin themes of family breakdown and moral decline were, however, attributed to other ideological agendas of the New Right. For example, in Britain the promotion of economic liberalism and the ideology of the free market as the answer to the industrial ills of the postwar period was founded on a new and more strident form of moral individualism. In the competitive, go-getter society of Thatcher's Britain and Reagan's America, success was measured increasingly in terms of personal acquisition and wealth (Holman 1993). Those who fell by the wayside in the wake of the government's budgetary reductions, or who failed to compete successfully in the marketplace, were regarded as whingers or, in Thatcher's words, 'moaning minnies.'

In order to justify the new reality, a moral interpretation of individual action was required. This was achieved through the promotion of the ideology of responsibility. Citizens could no longer expect benevolent handouts from the nanny state—they had to stand on their own two feet. People were regarded as responsible only if they could demonstrate a capacity for self-motivation and self-reliance.

The New Right's notion of responsibility, however, extended well beyond the terrain of free-market economics. It was also applied to other policy areas such as education and criminal justice. During the 1980s, for example, penal policy in Britain and America (and later, Australia) was increasingly based upon highly individualistic conceptions of crime and punishment. Offending behaviours were seen as resulting from the rational and calculating actions of individuals rather than from external sources such as unemployment and socioeconomic disadvantage (Hudson 1993). Offenders who failed to act responsibly, therefore, would be held directly accountable for their actions. As we argue in Chapter Three, the notion of responsibility has figured prominently in criminal justice discourse in a number of Western countries and has also been extended to the parents of juvenile offenders.

One of the major ironies of economic liberalism was that it generated even more of the social and economic conditions its reforms were designed to overcome. As Brake and Hale point out in relation to the Thatcher revolution in Britain: 'Ironically, with its determined attempt to restructure the economy at the expense of the working class, and by taking such a hard line on scroungers and loungers, the conservative Government has created the very social conditions which have led to the intensification of the very crime wave it was elected to end' (Brake and Hale, 1993: 171). Another consequence of the changes sweeping Britain and the United States during the 1980s and 1990s was the emergence of widespread and serious outbreaks of violence among the young in inner-citiy areas (Campbell 1994). Despite the appeal to a new moral order based on family values and tradition, it became increasingly clear that the structural conditions generated by radical market liberalism had sown the seeds for social unrest in the heartlands of British and American cities.

By the same token the emphasis given to the notion of responsibility and self-reliance led to a situation in which more and more families found it difficult to make ends meet (Cook 1997). Yet it was still relatively easy for governments to deflect criticism of their policies onto the urban poor. The creation of a moral climate based on rampant individualism meant that the problems faced by families and the crimes committed by their children could be attributed to moral failure rather than sociopolitical conditions (Brake and Hale 1993: 172). This ideological regime was further buttressed by the rise of conservative criminologies in which academic credence was given to rational-calculative theory and situational crime prevention. Crime control was thus reduced to the actuarial matter of designing out crime and ensuring that opportunities for offending were reduced to a bare minimum (Hudson 1996). As far as offenders were concerned, their actions were explained in terms of a conscious, premeditated calculation of the costs and benefits of crime (Hudson 1987). The task facing law enforcement agencies, therefore, was to keep a close watch on high crime areas and to ensure that appropriate penalties were applied to offenders and (increasingly) their parents. Ultimately, the responsibility for crime prevention was said to rest with the offender and his or her family. As Brake and Hale noted of the British government's approach to crime control in the 1980s, 'The basis of morality and law-abiding behaviour has become the family and it follows that parents must be made responsible for their children's misdemeanors' (1993: 172). The neutralizing of other social and economic explanations for offending behaviours was completed by rounding on those families who were seen as prime examples of dysfunction and failure. As Utting (1995: 13) notes in response to the blame being heaped upon the parents of juvenile offenders in Britain, '... when times are hard and policies prove impotent, few scapegoats are more easily grasped than the stubborn failure of some parents to raise successful, law abiding children at minimum cost to the state.' To be sure, in Australia, as in other western states, the situation facing many families has been such as to make it difficult to exercise good enough parenting. The observations of the Director of the Families in Stress Foundation in Melbourne, John Embling (1986), could well be applied to many thousands of families in contemporary Britain, America and Australia. '... increasing numbers of people's lives in our society were going badly wrong; not in a temporary way, as a result of a mistake, but because the basic structures that we take for granted—a reasonably secure home, competent schooling, the prospect of a decent job after school etc.—simply did not exist' (Embling 1986: 87). Moreover, as Anderson states: 'While politicians increasingly (during the 1970s and 1980s) urged parents to control their children more closely—part of the myth that in the past they had always succeeded in doing so—parents of teenagers had fewer usable material or cultural means for doing so' (Anderson 1994: 86).

Such matters did not appear to concern those who saw the problems besetting families as of their own making. Indeed, as Cass points out, in order to obviate reference to deep-seated structural inequalities, western governments called increasingly for a return to the traditional dependencies of family life. Thus:

> ... in a period of increasing rates of unemployment, increasing rates of change in household and family formation and increasing aging of the population—all generating a rise in the number of actual or potential welfare beneficiaries—and an increasing government commitment to restrain public expenditure for social purposes, one of the strategies available to governments is to encourage the privatization of welfare provision. Emphasis on the traditional dependencies of the family serves this purpose, by focusing attention on the proper role of families to care for their disadvantaged members. (Cass 1988: 23–4)

In the new moral climate of economic liberalism, parents were seen as playing a crucial role in the war against crime. At the same time, however, growing criticism was being levelled against single parents who were regarded as overly dependent upon the state (Young 1996). Despite the fact that households comprised of single mothers made up only a small percentage of all families, they nonetheless attracted sustained attacks from the media who regarded them as virtual social pariahs (Lister 1996; Pilger 1998). Teenage mothers in particular came to symbolize the demise of the traditional family and the slide into social disintegration. Their presence appeared to signal the widespread emergence of fatherless families which were unable (by definition) to provide the necessary moral frameworks for their children. In Britain during the early 1990s, links were drawn between the eruptions of inner-city violence by disaffected youths and the apparent absence of effective maternal care and supervision. As Beatrice Campbell observed, '[The old responsibility and the New Right] blame the mothers. The fact that communities and families do not ostracize or evict their criminalized children, or rather their sons, is forgotten in the lament interminably invoked, that Britain's poor places are impoverished because of the failure of the family' (Campbell 1994: 153). One of the most graphic illustrations of this alleged failure, seized upon by New Right pessimists, involved the brutal murder in 1992 in England of a nine-year-old boy, James Bolger (Morrison 1998). The conviction of two children for this offense was accompanied by claims that the breakdown of the family was singularly responsible for such horrendous crimes

(Francis 1993). Again, single mothers received much of the blame for this state of affairs (Young 1996). Their apparent failure to unite the household and to provide the necessary moral guidance for their children explained the increase in violent and other aberrant behaviours among the young. According to some commentators, the breakdown of the family, along with a popular culture based on violence and a disregard for moral authority, established the conditions in which crime and delinquency could flourish. The fact that crime was seen to be burgeoning in areas populated by the urban poor was regarded as further evidence that the family, or certain types of families, had lost control of their members. The inner-city riots of the late 1980s and early 1990s in Britain and America appeared to signal (at least to the powerful) that the crime problem was associated most closely with the actions of the young urban poor (Hudson 1993). At the same time it was possible to represent this population as somehow different to the rest of us, as a threat that had to be contained. In promoting the notion of an underclass, New Right commentators (such as Charles Murray and James Q. Wilson) were able to depict this population in terms of its supposed essential characteristics: high unemployment, intergenerational welfare dependency, family breakdown, and so forth. Increasingly in the public mind (and in the minds of policy makers), the underclass represented all that was wrong with present-day society. This substratum of the disaffected occupied an ideological space in which the various intersections of disadvantage and social problems seemed to collide all at once. By singling out a section of the population as in some way distinct from the rest of society, it was possible to talk about appropriate measures to tackle the potential threat it posed to social order (Bessant 1996a). Moreover, although the problems besetting the urban poor were material in nature, the threat had resulted, according to the New Right, from moral degeneracy (Abbott and Wallace 1992: 10–14).

The demise of the stable family thus appeared to signal a deep moral crisis in which the traditional structures of moral authority no longer held sway. In Britain such concerns led to calls by the then Prime Minister, John Major, for a 'Back to Basics' campaign that would reawaken the moral certainties associated with the traditional family (Lister 1996). Similarly, in the United States, the Republican inspired 'Focus on the Family' movement called for a return to traditional family values and a rolling back of the secularism and permissiveness of more recent times. In Australia, concerns over the family saw the establishment of the cross-party Lyon's Group which announced its intention to pursue family-based social policies.

The pessimistic concerns of such political movements also found expression in research findings published by neoconservative think tanks in Britain, the United States, and Australia (Azevado 1998). In the latter country, the Centre for Independent Studies (CIS), a self-described 'leading independent public policy research institute in Australia and New Zealand,' issued two major reports on rising levels of crime in Australia. The reports, 'Statistical Indicators of Australia's Well-Being' (1997a) and 'Rising Crime in Australia' (1997b), both cited in Centre for Independent Studies, generated considerable public debate, not least for their tendency to make sweeping generalizations about the alleged causes of crime. In eye-catching headlines such as 'Violent crime soars on par with family breakdown' (*Weekend Australian* July 5–6, 1997) and 'Violent crime wave swamps police capacity' (*The Australian* November 7, 1997) a grim picture was painted by the CIS of spiraling levels of crime throughout Australia, brought about chiefly by family breakdown and a chronic shortage of police officers.

Although such statistical speculations have been strongly challenged by statisticians, criminologists, and others, the fact that so much media attention has been devoted to the CIS studies indicates a readiness to entertain findings that supposedly link crime with family breakdown. Nevertheless, the also relevant fact that a vast body of research in the United States, Britain, and Australia shows that the so-called broken home cannot be linked directly to crime and that the quality of care provided to children is more important than family structure, has not lessened the focus on family breakdown as a key generator of crime (see Chapter Three in this volume; Utting 1994). The CIS studies rehearse a hackneyed and simplistic explanation of the origins of crime, namely, that the ultimate causes of such behaviour reside in the family context and are directly attributable to the absence of appropriate maternal care.

With an assumed link between families and crime, it is hardly surprising that there have been numerous calls for education programs aimed at enhancing parenting skills. In Britain, a Home Office Research Unit study (1994) called for the creation of open access family centers, parent support groups, and the provision of specialized counseling for those parents finding it difficult to cope with their children. In Australia, there have been calls for measures to support parents in times of crisis through the provision of family centers and various home supports in order to facilitate best-practice parenting. The pretext for such proposals has been the perception among professional workers and the wider public that parents are struggling to provide adequate care and control of their children. In an address to the Australian Institute of Criminology in September 1992, an educational counselor argued strongly that a range of measures were required if parents were to be more responsible and accountable. Amid talk of parents lacking the necessary motivation and skills to bring about a sense of social responsibility in their children, it was argued that community and government intervention was required to bring about effective parenting. This, it was argued, could provide 'consequent societal benefits including a reduction in the adult and juvenile crime rate' (Radford 1992: 2). Such prescriptions typify many of the individualistic discourses of juvenile crime since the 1980s. The problem of juvenile crime, as well as other social problems, is thus laid directly at the door of unskilled or inadequate parenting. Material considerations such as poverty, unemployment and deprivation and the changing nature of crime control in western countries play little or no part in such prescriptive accounts.

Conclusion

This chapter has sought to trace the elements of public discourse that have contributed to the view that the origins of crime are to be found in the family home. This theme has been repeated with monotonous regularity in recent years and is now firmly embedded in the criminal justice policies in a number of countries. We have argued that the emergence of the notion of parental responsibility has its roots in individualistic ideologies that have percolated into various aspects of social thought in recent decades. The family has been viewed as a conduit through which social order and integration can be achieved. Any threat to the stability of this institution is regarded as a threat to society itself. In the past few decades the perceived breakdown of the modern family has, according to some commentators, led to the rise of crime and delinquency among the young. Parents rather than governments have been held responsible for the collapse in moral authority. The task facing the state, therefore, is to ensure that responsibility and accountability is brought back home, where it belongs.

A major assumption underpinning recent news reports, police actions, and government policy is that juvenile crime results mainly from the failure of parents to adequately supervise their children. Such an assumption supports the importance of this project in seeking to understand the ways in which juvenile offending affects families. For instance, how do parents deal with the news that one (or more) of their children is in trouble with the police? What measures, if any, do parents and families take to deal with offending behaviours? What are the consequences for the family when a young person is criminalized? What do young people and their parents think about the interventions of criminal justice agencies? Can we simply assume that juvenile offending results from the actions of negligent parents? The indications from the present research are that juvenile crime has a number of far-reaching consequences for family members, including the offender. Whatever else parents might do in such situations, they are rarely indifferent to the consequences that offending and criminalization have on the family as a whole. As the accounts of family members in this study will show, the commission of offending by a young person may have life-altering consequences for the entire family. Indifference is not an option if the family is to address the negative impact of policing and criminalization upon the family.

CHAPTER THREE

Families and Juvenile Justice

Introduction

This chapter focuses on a range of developments in western states that have led to the growing absorption of the family into systems of juvenile crime control. The emergence of community control—an alliance of active citizens and state-sponsored control agencies—has led to the greater integration of the family, school, and neighbourhood into the culture of crime control. We argue, however, that this absorption into the system is achieved through a range of disciplinary measures designed to ensure the active compliance of parents in the management of their children. These measures have been legitimated by the state under the pretext of increasing personal and family responsibility.

The home front

The past twenty years or so have witnessed a number of fundamental changes to both the ideological foundations and disciplinary practices of western systems of juvenile crime control (Garland 1994). Such changes, however, have proceeded not by a smooth transition from one programmatic phase to another but rather through the gradual inclusion of new and recycled philosophies and practices (Hudson 1996: 1–13, see also Garland and Young 1983). The changes are also typified by considerable systemic confusion about how best to deal with crime. Indeed, retribution, treatment, reform, incapacitation, rehabilitation, and reintegration often occupy the same uneasy ideological terrain of crime management. It is often characteristic of systems of crime control that they come to embrace enlightened and more humanitarian approaches to crime management (usually by invoking the notion of community) while at the same time relying on antiquated penologies of punishment and retribution (Cohen 1984).

Given the fragmented evolution of crime control in western countries, it would be erroneous to claim the absolute ascendancy of one philosophy or practice over another. It has been argued, for instance, that there has over the years been a quantum shift from the justice to the welfare model of criminal justice (Pratt 1993). Closer examination of the system, however, reveals a more complex picture in which residues of previous practices are in fact integral to the day-to-day operations of criminal justice. Nonetheless, it is apparent that some significant changes to penal policy and practice have occurred in a number of western countries over recent years (Garland 1996). There is, for example, more talk of reintegration and restorative justice than of treatment and reform; and of justice in the community than of welfare intervention.

The ideology of restorative justice has been particularly evident in respect of the role played by families in both the prevention and adjudication of juvenile crime (Consedine 1995). Parents have been called upon by the state to participate more and more in a strategic, community wide response to juvenile crime. Battle lines are no longer drawn simply (in the classical Lombrosian sense) between the state and deviant populations but are distributed in countless localized sites of crime prevention and risk management (Feeley and Simon 1994).

Central to the development of community-based crime control has been the co-option of the family, school, and neighbourhood into various localized projects. Governments have called for active citizenship in an effort to combat growing social disorder, especially among juvenile populations. Parents have been urged to exhibit greater commitment to the care and control of their children, or face the possibility of official sanctions. If their children offend, parents may be required to participate actively in processes of conflict resolution as well as attempts to reintegrate the offender or at risk young person back into the community.

Putting family responsibility back into justice

As suggested in the previous chapter, the most unifying (and ideologically powerful) concept resonating through family-based crime control initiatives is that of responsibility. The idea of responsibility in criminal justice has its recent origins in the back to justice movement of the late 1960s. Based on the works of Von Hirsh (1976, 1993) and others, the movement espoused a legal philosophy that sought to remove some of the excesses of state intervention inherent in the so-called welfare model. The latter was seen by liberal and conservative critics alike as responsible for a growing number of unwarranted incursions by the state into the lives of offenders and their families. In the wake of growing criticism of welfarism by social scientists, liberal activists, and conservative politicians there developed a counterdiscourse in which the previous hegemony of welfarism was exposed for its overly intrusive and disciplinary practices. Parental rights and the rights of the child were promoted in opposition to the perceived interference by social workers, magistrates, and others (Rose 1990). Emphasis was placed increasingly on the autonomy of the family insofar as it was seen as the natural site for the governance of its potentially deviant members. The notion of privacy therefore came to signify a more responsible and independent approach to family life in which the previously sanctioned encroachments of outsiders were seen as counterproductive (Rose 1990: 203–5).

In an attempt to introduce a more standardized and equitable system of justice in which offenders could be dealt with according to their deeds rather than needs, proponents of the justice model argued that welfarism should be replaced by a system of justice that operationalized the principles of due process and proportionality (Naffine 1993). Such a system, it was argued, would guarantee that the focus of judicial attention was directed away from the social conditions associated with offending to the particular actions of the individual. Criminal action, therefore, was considered to result primarily from the failure of the offender to act responsibly. By the same token, offending was seen as a rational and calculating form of behaviour in which the individual had made a conscious choice to pursue a particular course of action for individual gain (O'Connor 1992). The individualistic philosophy underpinning the justice model thus contained within it a more precise focus on the calculated actions of the offender (Pratt 1993). Social conditions were no longer regarded as the sole or sufficient grounds for mitigation in court cases.

As noted in the previous chapter, the ascendancy of individualism in criminal justice dovetailed neatly with a range of conservative ideologies that came to prominence during the early 1980s. It was during this period that rational choice theory, as well as other criminological theories, merged with the penological individualism advocated by promoters of the justice model. The reassertion of neoclassical formulations of moral individualism led to the responsibilization of the crime problem in which the social fact of high crime was seen as the outcome of personal aberration rather than social malaise (Garland 1996. See also O'Malley 1996).

It is against this background of individualism that much of the current discourse on crime control needs to be understood. Although the notion of responsibility comes in various liberal and conservative guises, there nonetheless exists a shared assumption that the responsibility for crime and its prevention rests first and foremost with offenders and their families. The disciplinary strategies designed to achieve greater responsibility have also taken various forms. In their more liberal-humanitarian form, control initiatives are seen as a way of including the families of offenders and their families in the preventive project. On the other hand, the failure to act responsibly offers a convenient rationale for a range of penalties to be imposed on both the offender and his or her family.

Although the blaming of families for juvenile crime is hardly new, the current ethos of reponsibilization is distinguished by the particular configuration of crime management practices in a number of western countries. The dualistic (and often contradictory) approaches to crime management (punishment and retribution alongside restoration and prevention) have arisen through a complex range of ideologies, many of which have their origins in the patterns of crime control formed in preindustrial society. The current system, however, is distinguished by a number of ideological imperatives that seek to extend the boundaries of crime control from the centralized state apparatus to the community as a whole. The dispersal of control to the social body has occurred in large measure through a nostalgic appeal to the informal controls once exercised by the community. The current crime control agenda, however, with its increased focus on the agencies of the family, school, and neighbourhood, has developed mainly from a recognition that there are limits in the extent to which the state can control crime from the center. However, this is not so much a decentralizing process than the absorption of the community into the crime control culture via the participation of active citizens.

Families and community control

The limits to state sovereignty in respect of crime control have been the subject of considerable public debate over recent years (Garland 1996). The loss of public confidence in the police, continued low levels of clear-up, the rise of autonomous and extra-judicial forms of crime control (community action groups, vigilantism, and so forth) have contributed to a climate of public concern over the efficacy of law enforcement (Hogg and Brown 1998; Rose 1994). While many western governments have made bellicose statements about the need for tougher law and order measures in order to stem the rising tide of crime, their confidence and ability to achieve the desired level of social order has diminished. It is partly against this background that the movement towards community control has gathered pace over the past decade or so. Such developments have also emerged in response to a recognition (starting in the 1960s) that the criminal justice system, however well intentioned, tends to produce unforeseen consequences that worsen rather than alleviate the problem of crime. At the same time, public recognition of shortcomings in the system has been accompanied by what was widely seen as a more enlightened and progressive approach to the treatment of subject populations. Particular criticism has been directed at the areas of psychiatry and criminal justice on the grounds that institutionalized practices had resulted in a host of unintended consequences (mortification of self, institutionalization, systems abuse, prisons as human warehouses and schools of crime, overcrowding, recidivism, and so forth). The drive towards community care, alternatives to custody and policies and practices of reform, rehabilitation and (most notably) reintegration were symptomatic of the destructuring tendencies during this period (Cohen 1994).

At the heart of such developments was the ideological reliance upon the notion of community. Crime, it was argued, needed to be addressed through the unified efforts of various institutions in the community. People had to take responsibility for their own affairs. To assist this process in the 1970s, there emerged an army of youth workers, community workers and social-welfare practitioners dedicated to the task of strengthening community ties and ensuring that families were better placed to achieve their desired levels of autonomy. Very often, of course, nostalgia for the integrated community tended to gloss over the postwar realities that contributed to its apparent decline: unplanned development, environmental decay, high unemployment, inner-city violence, and growing poverty (Campbell 1994).

The key agencies identified by the state in terms of the dispersal of control were the family, school, and neighbourhood. Growing emphasis was placed on the role that such agencies could play in the war against crime. The rise of localized initiatives such as Neighbourhood Watch and Crime Stoppers, as well as prime-time television crime watch programs, were indicative of the new community orientation to crime. Other initiatives, such as the police-sponsored Blue Light Discos, Police Youth Clubs, Adopt-a-Cop and buddy systems, were seen as ways of forging closer links between the police and citizens (Hil 1996). Calls were made for a return to community policing and for increased educational and preventive involvement of police officers in schools.

The strengthening of ties between the community and law enforcement agencies was, according to Cohen (1985), reflective of a more penetrative and incisive extension of social control into the heartlands of problem areas. Such control was inclusive rather than exclusive and involved the voluntary and/or coerced participation of an active citizenry in the war against crime. Central to this strategy was

> . . . a greater direct involvement of the family, school and various community agencies in the day-to-day business of prevention, treatment and socialisation. But this is different than simply recruiting more volunteers, improving communication with schools or encouraging citizens to report more crime . . . Parents, peers, schools, the neighbourhood, even the police should dedicate themselves to keeping the deviant out of the formal system. Together they should constitute a giant shield of diversion: deflecting, absorbing, integrating the deviant back to the community where he belongs. (Cohen 1985: 77–8)

The family therefore came to play a central role in community control ideology. The home was regarded as one of the primary sites in which the at risk or actual offender could be integrated or even reintegrated into the community. Parents thus came to represent the principal guarantors of the child's moral character. The family was represented as a halfway house of socialization straddling the private authority of the home with the expectations of a state determined to ensure public compliance and social order. (For an earlier elaboration of this thesis, see Donzelot 1979). The management of offending, mainly through its preventative aspect, was thus devolved onto the shoulders of family members with the expectation that they could be held directly accountable when things went wrong. Families were granted an autonomy previously denied to them under the auspices of a welfare oriented state: 'They (schools, families, neighbourhoods) and not the experts and professionals must take responsibility for delivering control. Instead of depriving them of their potential, they should be strengthened and used as natural resources in the war against crime' (Cohen 1985: 77). Although the family was encouraged to take on a more active role in respect of its members, it was only particular family forms that were suited to the functions of socialization. For the traditionalists, it was the normal family, the heterosexual and domesticated nuclear family, rather than the broken, incomplete, or dysfunctional household, that was to lead the crusade against crime (Hil 1998). Accordingly, the task facing the state was to provide the necessary conditions in which the normalization of family forms could take place. Only in this way could families gain the necessary strength to enable them to participate effectively in the control and management of its potentially deviant members.

When problems in the process of normalization arose, however, the state would be required to intervene. Social management of dysfunctional families could therefore be used to bring about normalization ostensibly through the mediums of education and treatment. These interventions were legitimated on the grounds that the family is either engaged in damaging practices (abuse, neglect, lack of parental supervision/ control/discipline, and so forth) or that parents simply lack the required level of parenting skills. However, families failing to live up to social expectations are subject to varying degrees of surveillance and control by welfare and other officials. As Carrington points out, state intervention occurs most regularly and intensively in those families who are regarded as posing the most direct threat to social order:

> Child abuse, juvenile delinquency, truancy and parental incompetence provide socially acceptable routes for state intervention, whereby children can be removed from families and placed under state supervision under the pretext of the liberal state. So the autonomy of the family comes to depend not on legal rights, but on competence. Families in working class areas and Aboriginal communities enjoy loosely supervised freedom provided they meet certain basic social expectations about sending their children to school and controlling their public behaviour. However, some families are more loosely supervised than others. Aboriginal families and families from Housing Commission areas have borne the brunt of punitive child protection policies directed by incompetent parents and bad mothers under the pretext of saving children. (Carrington 1992: 117)

This emphasis on incompetence as a means of assessing the capacity of parents to care for their children is exhibited clearly in court cases involving juvenile offenders. For example, in a study of 124 presentence reports submitted to the Victoria Children's Court during 1990, it was found that child care officers tended to dwell on the psychological make-up of parents, or on their capacity to exercise particular caring skills. Consequently, the offending of the child tended to be explained by the perceived incompetence or negligence of parents in respect of their children. Similarly, young people from particular social backgrounds were also likely to be labeled in negative terms. Therefore, '. . . youths who are from predominantly working class backgrounds, poor families, single families and the socially disadvantaged are the most likely group of individuals to be labelled bad; because they do not conform to the notion of the traditional family and are thus expected to change their behaviours in order to be given control of their children. The result is an increased form of social control until the family is seen as able to take over completely the monitoring of the young person' (Simpson 1991: 81). The monitoring of various parental practices is, of course, part and parcel of a general approach to ensure the normalization of the potential deviant so as to reduce the element of threat to the wider community. Ultimately the aim of reintegrating the offender into the community is strategized in terms of the requirement of families and other social institutions to take control of their own members.

Bifurcatory practices

The approaches to crime control in western countries are many and varied. In Australia, for example, governments in a number of states and territories have developed strategies that encompass both preventative and punitive orientations. On the one hand, western governments have embraced community-based strategies that engage liberal and humanitarian ideas of restoration and reintegration while, on the other, courts have been granted powers to punish the negligent parents of juvenile offenders (see Chapter Nine for an analysis of parental restitution measures). In the remainder of this chapter we focus on a number of community-based measures that have given emphasis to the family in the war against crime. Specifically, we focus on family conferencing, community panels, curfews and crime prevention measures. While such approaches differ in terms of theory and practice, they nonetheless share some common assumptions about the role of families in the culture of crime control.

Conferencing

The conferencing model is one of the most significant developments in western juvenile crime control over the past decade or so. Broadly speaking, conferencing involves the active participation of the offender, his or her family, the victim, and a police or welfare officer in an open process of conflict resolution. The aim is not simply to provide restitution or compensation to the victim but also to engage the family and the offender in a process designed to shame and/or reintegrate the offender back into the community (Maxwell and Morris 1993). As such, conferencing is viewed as a way of both healing the effects of crime (Consedine 1995) and ensuring that the family is actively involved in the criminal justice process (Maxwell and Morris 1993: xvii). The conferencing model has thus come to symbolize the more humane and sensitive face of juvenile justice. Although not without its problems (and critics), conferencing has been warmly greeted by crime control managers in a number of countries. It has been described as an innovative, progressive, exciting approach to justice that both protects the offender from the damaging consequences of the usual formal process as well as offering some recompense to the victim (see Maxwell and Morris 1993; Alder and Wundersitz 1994). Such claims have attracted widespread attention from academics, politicians and policy makers who see conferencing as a new, family-based approach to criminal justice. As we will see, however, others are a little more skeptical about the claims associated with conferencing.

The impetus for the conferencing model came from some groundbreaking reforms in New Zealand during the late 1980s. In 1989 the New Zealand government legislated for fundamental changes to the juvenile justice system. Central to this was the introduction of Family Group Conferences (FGC) as part of a package of measures designed to operationalize the goals of diversion, accountability, due process, consensus decision making, cultural appropriateness and victim and family involvement (Maxwell and Morris 1993: xvi-xix). Based on Maori approaches to conflict resolution, FGCs were seen as a means by which the offender, her/his family and the victim could gather together to discuss the nature of the offense, its consequences, and possible ameliorative measures. FGCs, according to the New Zealand model, were regarded as a way of integrating the hitherto marginalized family into the decision-making process of the juvenile justice system.

In Australia various conferencing models are currently in operation across a number of states and territories. Although FGCs are regarded by some as a major new diversionary process and a means of empowering victims and families in the criminal justice system, they have also been subject to criticism on a number of grounds. Research in New Zealand indicates that the outcomes of FGCs often tend to be more punitive than the sentences handed out by the court system (Maxwell and Morris 1993). Further, while some victims benefit from the FGC process in terms of either confronting the perpetrator or in exacting compensation, others feel traumatized and distressed. Evidence also indicates that significant numbers of victims fail to attend FGC sessions (Maxwell and Morris 1993). Other critics point to the heavy involvement of the police in both the FGC process and the fact that the main focus is on the offender's deeds rather than her/his needs (Sandor 1994), thereby reinforcing an individualistic approach to the proceedings.

More fundamental criticisms have been aimed at the conferencing model. It is argued, for instance, that families and offenders are abstracted from the wider contexts of crime creation. As Ken Polk (1994: 130) remarks: 'They (FGCs) are not interventions which assume that the locus of the intervention should be within such institutions as work, school, politics, recreation, housing or health.' Other critics point to the victim blaming the nature of FGCs and their tendency to place the responsibility for offending squarely onto the shoulders of offenders and their families (White 1994: 189). In this sense the FGC operates as a quasi-judicial forum in which collectively agreed sentences can be handed out. The notion of parental responsibility is central to this process and is expressed ritualistically under the pretext of reintegrative shaming (Braithwaite 1989). The process of shaming, however, extends implicitly beyond the offender per se to the family as a whole. In having to adjudicate on its own misfortune, it is assumed that the family is best placed (and willing) to engage in disciplinary practices that are often alien to its own orientations. Despite the support and preparation given to participants in the process, the fact remains that conferencing is a formal process that compels the family to undertake action in respect of one or more of its deviant members.

It has also been argued that the ceremonial aspects associated with conferencing may have little relevance for indigenous people (who tend to make up disproportionate numbers of those embroiled in western systems of criminal justice). For example, the application of a repackaged communitarian form of conferencing, adapted from specific indigenous practices in New Zealand, may not be culturally appropriate to Australia's Aboriginal people (Blagg 1997). Furthermore, the appropriation of a model, designed to reclaim those indigenous children subject to practices under colonial rule, reflects an ideology of orientalism that effectively homogenizes those populations for whom conferences are intended (Blagg 1997). Conferencing may also possess an exotic aura in that the practices of indigenous people are idealized, repackaged, and applied mainly by non-Iindigenous architects of crime control to western systems of justice.

Leaving aside the ideological and epistemological ferment generated by conferencing, it is nonetheless clear that this approach to juvenile justice takes as its starting point the assumption that the family should be centrally involved in the judicial process. The rhetoric associated with conferencing also reflects many other areas of criminal justice discourse in which emphasis is given to the notion of responsibility as it relates to the adjudication of criminal action. Perhaps more than any other initiative, conferencing symbolizes the devolutionary practices of current crime control and the central stress placed on the family in this regard.

Panels

Another forum in which families have been involved is that of community panels. Over the last few years panels of various types have emerged across a number of western liberal states (Nichols 1985). Although concerned with diverse age groups of juvenile, young, and adult offenders at different stages in the criminal justice process (pre- or postcourt), panels are regarded as a way of engaging the family in a less formal judicial setting. The relative informality of proceedings, usually attended by the offender, her or his family and representatives of the community, is also seen as providing a setting in which participants can discuss solutions to criminal behaviour and even plan for the offender's future. The welfarism adopted by some panels, with their focus on the needs of the offender, is usually accompanied by an element of coercion aimed at ensuring the compliance of the offender and his or her parents. In the following example, we illustrate the ways in which a community panel was perceived by its often highly skeptical participants. It becomes clear that the good intentions of the panel members are experienced quite differently by offenders and their families.

The Townsville Youth Assistance Panel (YAP) was founded by the local Juvenile Aid Bureau of the Queensland Police Service in 1990. The aim was to offer offenders and their families the opportunity of resolving some of their difficulties outside the formal legal process, thus (hopefully) diverting offenders from the negative and stigmatizing processes of the court system. The panel also sought to offer participants advice and assistance in obtaining voluntary work or information about education and training courses in local colleges. The panel met every two weeks in the boardroom of a local business and was made up of prominent community representatives, mainly police officers, an attorney, and members of local service clubs. After hearing from the offender (invariably a petty first-time offender) and her/his family, and following some informal discussion (which, in fact, turned out to be more of a question-answer session) the panel decided in the presence of the family on an appropriate course of action.

Research into the operation of the panel revealed a number of complaints from participants about the excessive formality of proceedings and the general tone of authoritarianism exhibited by panel members (Hil 1994). Parents also felt excluded from the process and complained that little attention was given to the problems facing the family as a whole. The proceedings were likened to a court process and both offenders and their parents complained of feelings of powerlessness as well as of the patronizing approach of some panel members. There was also a marked degree of uncertainty in proceedings. Panel members often asked intrusive questions, the significance of which could only be guessed at by parents and their children. While parents were given an opportunity to speak, the invitation was issued in an almost inquisitorial fashion. Indeed, the social status of panel members, their links to the formal justice system, their standing in the local community, and the fact that they donned relatively formal dress (shirts, ties, business suits, and so forth) alienated them from the families. The presence of service club members lent an air of philanthropy to the proceedings. The offer of a job in a community program, invariably managed or owned by one of the service club members, was conferred with the expectation that due thanks would be received. Although parents were indeed grateful for the helpfulness and kindness of panel members, a strong element of coercion was built into the proceedings. It was made clear to participants from the outset that the failure of either parents or the young person to comply with the requirements of the panel could be used as information for the Children's Court should the offender re-appear. This provision inevitably shaped the nature of the proceedings. The compliance of the parents, their unquestioning approach to proceedings and the grateful acknowledgment of services offered were all influenced by the implicit compulsion associated with the proceedings. Thus, despite the informality associated with this community initiative, it was apparent that strong links existed with the formal legal process. The claim that the panel members were representative of the community was also subject to some skepticism. (The fact that there were no Indigenous panel members was significant in itself). Moreover, the somewhat self-conscious philanthropy of panel members was in fact perceived by young people and their families as based upon some quasi-judicial and coercive assumptions. In general, therefore, while the YAP was touted by the local Juvenile Aid Bureau as an alternative to the formal legal process, its actual operation betrayed a less informal and community based approach than was first thought. Indeed, the composition of the panel and its philanthropic ethos, while guaranteeing the compliance of young people and parents, were rarely viewed as a way of addressing the particular needs of families.

Although the YAP constitutes only one small-scale and local example of this type of informal initiative, it nonetheless reveals some of the problems which beset other community-based initiatives. The aim of involving the family in the resolution of the child's offending, although laudable, was not realized in the case of YAP. Instead, what emerged was an uneasy acquiescence on the part of the offender and his or her family in the face of some coercion. Like other such initiatives, YAP is reflective of the wider ideological developments currently shaping the crime control culture in Australia and elsewhere. Like FGCs, panels embrace the family as a key institution in the reintegrative process. The active participation of family members is seen as crucial in dealing with the young person's offending. The inclusion of families in such initiatives rests on the assumption that crime originates in the family context and that its prevention depends on the ability and/or willingness of parents to exercise proper supervision and control over their children.

Curfews

Curfews are usually systematic and organized attempts to limit the time and space of young people in public areas. They arise most often because of specific concerns about children and young people roaming the streets at night and/or about rising levels of crime in particular localities. Over recent years curfews have been established in numerous towns and cities. Although not necessarily a formal part of the juvenile justice system, they nonetheless complement a range of policing strategies aimed at dealing with local youth-related matters: They send a clear message to families and communities that young people should not be present in public areas at certain times. Curfews endorse the idea that children and young people should remain at home under the direct supervision of their parents. Invariably, when children do breach curfew orders, it is the parents who are most directly blamed. As Simpson and Simpson (1993: 1978) point out,

> Curfews provide a mechanism whereby families can be regulated through the manner in which they reinforce a particular view of

appropriate family behaviour. It is implicit in the concept of a curfew that parents are expected to keep their children indoors after dark and that they are responsible for their behaviour. Thus the use of curfews constructs the discourse surrounding the role of the family. Notions of increased family responsibility become the focus of debate at the expense of acknowledging structural inequalities which perpetuate perceived family failure.

It is in this sense of reinforcing specific notions of family responsibility that curfews share many of the assumptions of other family-based crime control measures. The message is repeated that it is the family that must take primary and direct responsibility for its members and that parents are held accountable when their children offend. Thus, like FGCs and panels, curfews set the context in which families are absorbed ever more deeply into the crime control culture. This is achieved through implicit moral strictures on aberrant parental practices as well as the threat of sanctions (shaming, financial penalties, and so forth) when their children offend.

Conclusion

Although Cohen's thesis of community control has been subject to criticism on the grounds that it fails to take account of the use of a wide range of penalties in the criminal justice system (Bottoms 1989), and for presenting an overly pessimistic view of social control in the modern state (Pratt 1993, Blagg and Smith 1989), it nonetheless succeeds in identifying some significant changes to the control apparatus in western countries in recent decades. These developments have been brought about by a host of factors, not least the demonstrable failure of the liberal state to meet its own objectives of crime control. The family, along with the school and the neighbourhood, have been increasingly absorbed into various aspects of crime management. This absorption has been accomplished by appealing to notions of community, by exhorting parents to become more active in the supervision of their children, and by presenting the threat of sanctions to parents who fail to comply with these demands of active citizenship. The disciplinary nexus imposed on the family, however, varies according to each predisposing ideology, whether it be restitution, reintegration, restorative justice, or crime prevention. Either way, the family is required to play a major role in the resolution of the offending of their children.

Chapter Four

Researching Families of Juvenile Offenders

The attention given to the family in crime control discourse has been more than matched by the prolonged gaze of empirical researchers. Every facet of family life—its form, structure, dynamic—has been put under the methodological microscope in an effort to establish the precise causes of juvenile crime. In this chapter, we argue that studies of families and crime have been characterized largely by their individualistic orientation. This is hardly surprising since many of these studies are located squarely in the paradigm of developmental psychology. What concerns researchers is not the abstract business of theorizing the various forces that contribute to the creation of crime and delinquency but rather the identification of factors or predictive indicators that may be correlated with such behaviours. We maintain that despite the occasional nod towards environmental or background factors—including issues such as unemployment, poverty, institutionalized disadvantage, racism, policing, and so forth—most empirical studies in this area tend to equate crime with the internal workings of family life.

Early studies of families and crime

The post-Second World War period saw the ascendancy of psychological theories of child development and personality. The works of Freud and other psychoanalysts continued to have a profound influence on the way in which studies on children and families were conducted. Two of the most influential writers during the 1940s and 1950s were British psychologists Donald Winnicott and John Bowlby. The contributions of these researchers had a considerable impact on the theory and practice of child care and welfare, particularly in respect of those children who displayed maladjusted and/or antisocial behaviours.

At the heart of both Bowlby's and Winnicott's work was the assumption that the deprivation of maternal love and warmth in early childhood was likely to produce all manner of problematic attitudes and behaviours in the child. This thesis was elaborated by Winnicott in a number of books, including *The Child, the Family and the Outside World* (1968) and *The Family and Individual Development* (1964). A summary of his views on the links between family relationships and delinquency was published posthumously in an edited volume entitled *Deprivation and Delinquency* (1984). In the text of a speech given to English magistrates in 1946, Winnicott articulated his hope that courts would use psychological methods to investigate the causes of offending. This was grounded in the belief that the origins of delinquency were to be found in the disruptions to parent/child relations during the formative years. Delinquency was thus viewed as a consequence of the instability brought about by an absence of controls in the normal stages of emotional growth. The antisocial child begins to look beyond the family milieu in order to obtain the sense of emotional security denied by his/her immediate family. The delinquent act is a search for maternal love. As Winnicott (1984: 116) states: 'When a child steals outside his own home he is still looking for his mother, but he is seeking with more sense of frustration, and increasingly needing to find at the same time the parental authority that can and will put a limit to the actual effect of his impulsive behaviour, and to the acting out of the ideas that come to him when he is in a state of excitement.' Unlike the normal child, the antisocial delinquent requires intervention in the form of personal psychotherapy or a strong stable environment full of love and warmth if the necessary internal constraints are to be instilled (Winnicott 1983: 117–8).

For John Bowlby, the deprivation of maternal love and the consequent loss of attachment, particularly in the child's first five years, was considered central to any explanation of delinquency. This argument was repeatedly articulated in a range of books spanning a 30-year period. In perhaps his best known book, *Child*

Care and the Growth of Love, Bowlby argued that the prolonged separation of the child from his/her mother (or mother substitute) during the first five years 'stands foremost among the causes of delinquent character development' (1953: 44). The assertion is supported in Bowlby's study of forty-four thieves. In comparing this group with a control group of similar age and sex, it was found that the former included many more of those described as 'affectionless characters.' According to Bowlby, many of them had experienced prolonged periods of separation from their mothers (or foster mothers) during the early years. Those with the most frequent and prolonged periods of maternal deprivation displayed the most severe signs of delinquency (Bowlby 1953).

Winnicott's and Bowlby's assertions that the origins of delinquency were located in quite specific relationships between children and their parents (or substitute parents) had a lasting influence on generations of social welfare workers. Their works affirmed a link between the experiences of children in the early formative years and later tendencies towards antisocial behaviour. The dominance of individualistic theory in the areas of child and family welfare during the 1940s and 1950s meant that the deprivation theses of Winnicott and Bowlby had a ready audience among those professional groups concerned with the treatment of young offenders (Rose 1990).

Despite the initial popularity of both Winnicott's and Bowlby's works, criticism was increasingly aimed at the simplistic and assumptive nature of their conclusions. The most forceful criticism of Bowlby's work is found in Michael Rutter's book, *Maternal Deprivation Reassessed* (1972). In drawing on extensive psychological research, Rutter mounted a devastating attack on the maternal deprivation thesis. He argues that Bowlby (like Winnicott) tended to promote single cause explanations of complex issues such as juvenile delinquency. Rutter also asserted that the maternal deprivation thesis rested on a number of unwarranted assumptions about the nature of family life, particularly in respect of the bonding between mother and child. According to Rutter, the deleterious influences upon a child cannot be simply traced to either the mother or to deprivation: 'While loss is probably an important factor in one of the syndromes associated with "maternal deprivation," a review of the evidence suggests that in most cases the damage comes from "lack" or "distortion" of care rather than any form of "loss"' (Rutter 1972: 123). Moreover, Rutter states that '... it is not maternal bonding that needs to be studied but rather the nature of the relationship itself.... It should be appreciated that the chief bond need not be with a biological parent, it need not be with the chief caretaker and it need not be with a female' (Rutter 1972: 126–127). Similarly, as Utting, Bright, and Henricson (1994: 20) point out, analysis of parent-child relationships should focus not on the presence of a particular carer but rather on the quality of care experienced by the child.

Another criticism of Bowlby's work is the emphasis given to the role of mothers in the child rearing process. It is argued, for example, that the notion of bonding rests on some quite specific deterministic assumptions about the natural role of women in the process of child rearing. Feminist critics argue that such a view ignores the socially constructed nature of motherhood and the way in which women are positioned in terms of their reproductive roles and functions (see Naffine 1997). Although Bowlby offered a more complex explanation of motherhood and bonding than that often suggested by his critics, a somewhat simplistic rendition of the deprivation thesis was nonetheless absorbed by generations of child care 'experts' (Rutter 1972: 127).

In the United States, one of the first major studies to focus on family relationships and delinquency was undertaken by Harvard criminologists Sheldon and Eleanor Glueck. In their longitudinal study of more than 500 officially defined delinquent boys matched with nondelinquent boys from Boston, the Gluecks assembled a vast range of social, psychological, and biological data aimed at identifying the particular characteristics of the delinquent. The results of their research, published in *Unraveling Juvenile Delinquency* (1950), demonstrated the apparent link between family functioning and juvenile delinquency. The Gluecks argued that delinquent behaviour could be predicted by a number of key factors, including the extent to which the boy was disciplined by the father; the nature of mother's supervision of the boy; the extent of affection of the father and mother for the boy; and the general 'cohesiveness of the family' (Glueck and Glueck 1950: 261). At the center of their explanation of crime therefore was the assumption that internal workings of the family were primarily responsible for the onset of such behaviours. The actions of offenders were therefore directly attributable to the dysfunctional dynamics of family life.

Although such conclusions were highly influential, they soon attracted criticism, mainly on theoretical and methodological grounds. In an analysis of the Gluecks' data, Laub and Sampson (1988: 360) identified a number of shortcomings in the Boston study. The most serious of these was the general lack of systematic attention to the influence of socioeconomic factors on delinquency and the failure to acknowledge the processes by which offenders were officially defined as such. Thus, according to Laub and Simpson, the Gluecks' work was rather superficial insofar as it ignored the complex ways in which external factors influenced young people and their families. Despite such reservations, however, Laub and Sampson (1988: 375) proceeded to support the central contention of the Gluecks that family process variables (supervision, attachment, and discipline) comprised the most important factors in explaining delinquency. Such support for the Gluecks' work is perhaps not surprising given the strong appeal of family factors in explanations of juvenile crime. As we demonstrate below, the internal workings of the family continue to provide researchers with a host of factors that can be easily linked to juvenile crime. The positivist impulse evident in many of these works means that the awkward business of theorizing the contexts of offending behaviours and reactions to them is ignored entirely or relegated to the shadowy status of background factors.

The pathological family

Since Bowlby, Winnicott, and the Gluecks, there has been a proliferation of studies focusing on the links between families and crime. While factors such as unemployment, urban decay, poor education, and housing are seen to have some bearing on the onset of offending, it is the internal dynamics of family life that receive most empirical attention. In general reviews of the causes of crime, regular links have been drawn between family functioning and the onset of delinquency. In America, for example, a prominent criminologist, James Q. Wilson, has elaborated a distinctly pathological account of offending behaviour which he attributes directly to the 'deep-seated temperamental problems' exhibited by parents who 'lack much desire to change their children's behaviour' (Wilson and Herrnstein 1985: 366). Similarly, in a review of American and British studies of families and crime, psychologist Patricia Morgan concludes that the origins of criminal behaviour among the young are to be found in 'quarreling, discordant homes with violent or insane parents' or in 'disharmonious families' where there was 'tension' or a 'lack of warmth' (Morgan 1978: 94). The fact that such conclusions are drawn from empirical studies conducted over more than half a century reflects the particular theoretical orientations of such investigations. We see in Morgan's assertions, for instance, echoes of the deprivation theses articulated in earlier works by Winnicott and Bowlby. In asserting that crime can be linked explicitly to particular types of relationships within the family it is possible to go a step further and distinguish certain families in terms of their dysfunctional and/or criminogenic features. Indeed, the assertions contained in academic literature often bear a striking similarity to more popular ideas about the failing or dysfunctional family found in public discourse on crime and delinquency (Cook 1997).

The efforts to identify the role of family factors in the creation of delinquency has been exhaustive. Indeed, Wells and Rankin (1986: 87) note that during the 1980s in the United States, at least 65 major studies were conducted on the relationship between broken families and crime. Other inquiries (mainly in America and Britain) have attempted to correlate a wide range of family factors with the onset of delinquency, including parental neglect and abuse, divorce, separation, and bereavement (the broken home); the presence of latch-key children; the emergence of working mothers; lack of love, attachment, closeness; and family size (Rigoli and Hewitt 1991: 181–206).

The sheer volume of studies in this area is testament to the extraordinary aetiological focus given to the family. However, as will be shown below, the conclusions stemming from these inquiries are narrow and inconsistent. Moreover, the individualistic orientation of many inquiries in this area has meant that little or no effort has been devoted to critical examination of terms such as crime and delinquency or to the general processes by which particular individuals are labeled as such. Indeed, the atheoretical nature of these studies means that their ability to explain the connections between families and crime is severely limited.

The broken family

Typically referred to in terms of the absence of a parent through divorce, separation or bereavement, the broken home or broken family has attracted the most persistent attention among empirical researchers concerned with families and crime. Such interest is partly attributable to the general persuasiveness of the maternal deprivation thesis (Utting 1994) and to the popular belief that the broken home *per se* leads to antisocial behaviours among the young (Young 1996).

In a meta-analysis of 65 American studies of broken homes and delinquency, it was found that the correlation was 'stronger for minor forms of juvenile misconduct (status offenses) and weakest for serious forms of criminal behaviour' (Wells and Rankin 1986: 87). It was further concluded that broken homes produced slightly higher levels of delinquency among children when compared to the results of intact family households. Also, the type of break-up in households tended to affect levels of delinquency. Thus, 'delinquency is slightly stronger for families broken by divorce and separation than by the death of a parent' (Wells and Rankin 1991: 89).

In one of the largest American studies of juvenile misconduct and the broken home in which two national samples totaling 2,242 children were analyzed, psychologist John Rankin found that broken homes correlated significantly only with three types of self-reported juvenile misconduct: running away from home, truanting and fighting. Even in these cases, however, it was difficult to state with any certainty whether such outcomes were directly related to family structure. Indeed, Rankin concludes that 'the relationship between broken homes and running away and truancy do not seem particularly strong' (Rankin 1983: 478). This conclusion has been supported in other general reviews of the literature in this area. Thus, the relationship between broken families and delinquency has been described as 'weak' (Rigoli and Hewitt 1991: 206), 'less than convincing' (Jeffs and Smith 1990: 35) or as 'not at all strong' (Lowry 1994: 6). More importantly, however, is the failure of empirical studies to consider the broader sociological factors associated with families and crime. As Wells and Rankin (1986: 8) point out: 'Despite the sizable body of empirical research extending back to the turn of the century the 'broken home' question remains unsettled and ambiguous. A major shortcoming in the literature is the virtual absence of any systematic conceptual specification and corresponding empirical measurement of the broken home as a sociological variable. Although it seems straightforward on its face, more careful analysis reveals it to be a summary gloss for a multiplex combination of family structural and interactional conditions.' It is thus apparent that rather than offering any firm conclusions on the etiology of offending, the empirical focus on family structure has blurred the importance of other factors both in and out the family-household. As Utting (1993: 20) rightly points out: 'Family structure—in this instance being raised in a one-parent family—may be of less direct significance than the quality of care and supervision that individual parents are able to provide.' The ability of parents to provide good quality care and supervision is influenced by such factors as the presence of poverty, unemployment, low income, or racism (see Holman 1995). Thus, in seeking to provide families with the practical means of assistance to deal with delinquency, it may be far more productive to address questions of low income and deprivation than family structure (Utting, Bright, and Henricson 1994: 22).

Sibling numbers

Family size, usually measured in terms of the number of siblings, features repeatedly in empirical investigations of families and crime. However, as with the broken family, the link between the number of siblings in a household and delinquency is, at best, weak. In a longitudinal British study it was found that although large family size was correlated with delinquency, this factor was secondary to the nature and quality of family relations, particularly between children and parents (Farrington 1994: 14–15). Similarly, an American study found only a tenuous relationship between family size and delinquency. It was concluded that '... the home environment may be more important than family structure variables such as size for some youths' (Leflore 1988: 639). The personal growth and general maturity of children in terms of their abilities to relate to others were regarded as far more important than the number of siblings at home. Having said this, the pressures posed by very large families had a marked impact on the ability of parents to care adequately for their children (Leflore 1988: 640). In another American study, for example, a connection was found between larger families and the reduced ability of parents to supervise their children adequately (Tygart 1991: 535). This study also concluded, however, that it is difficult to separate the question of family size per se and its impact on delinquency from other considerations such as peer group influence and school experience. Generally, the assumption of a close connection between family size and offending is largely unfounded (Rutter and Giller 1983: 109). At best, family size may be considered as one of a range of influences that may, or may not, have a bearing upon the emergence of delinquency (Utting 1994: 18–19).

The failing family

One of the major conclusions to emerge from a large number of studies in this area is that the quality of family relationships is far more important than issues of size and structure (Junger-Tass 1994: 23). This point has been recognized by researchers who over the past few years have turned their considerable empirical gaze upon the quality of parent–child relations and its effects on crime. Again, much of this research can be linked to earlier deprivation theses in which the relationship between parents and their children was seen to have a direct bearing upon the development of the child. A major implication stemming from such approaches is that the onset of crime can be attributed to the evident failings in parent–child relations. Parental failure is thus exhibited in poor emotional relationships between parents and their children and in the inability of parents to exercise effective child-rearing skills.

In a longitudinal study of over 400 working class British boys, Farrington (1994: 12–15) argues that inconsistent and poor parenting has a direct bearing on the emergence of delinquency. Parental attitudes and the quality of supervision and discipline are considered vital in preventing the onset of antisocial behaviour. Farrington reaches a number of stark and simplistic conclusions about the relationship between parenting and delinquency. For example: '. . . parents who let their children roam the streets unsupervised from an early age tend to have delinquent children'; or, '. . . warm, loving parents tend not to have delinquent children, while cool, rejecting parents tend to have delinquent children.' 'Erratic and inconsistent discipline' is also considered a major cause of delinquency (Farrington 1994: 10).

Such conclusions have been replicated in a recent Australian study of young offenders in three Queensland centers: Cairns, Mackay, and Brisbane. Following extensive interviews with over 1000 young people aged between 13 and 18 years, the team of researchers from Queensland University of Technology concluded that:

> The results show that the quality of the relationship between youth and their parents was consistently much poorer for offending youth compared to the sample as a whole. This was also reflected in the degree of support that young people felt they could draw on at home. Those who had offended felt much less support than youth generally. The responses to questions about family conflicts, violence, fear of getting hurt, alcohol, and drugs being associated with fights supported the reporting of poorer parental relationships. (Thomas, Heim, and O'Connor 1993: 10. See also Thomas and Heim 1993a, 1993b)

According to the researchers, such conclusions seem to support earlier studies that show that offending is strongly influenced by the distant emotional relationship between parents and their children and poor or low levels of parental supervision (Thomas et al. 1993).

A recent British study of 2,528 young people aged between 14 and 25 also found a close connection between offending and poor quality family relationships. It was concluded that low levels of parental supervision were closely dependent upon the quality of parent-child relationships, particularly between children and fathers. Graham and Bowling (1996: xii) note that: 'Both males and females who were less attached to their families were more likely to offend than those who were relatively content at home.' The study identified low parental supervision and truancy as key factors in offending behaviour among the majority of young people in the sample.

Such studies suggest a close connection between various emotional deprivations in parenting practices and a lack of appropriate skills. Such skills are said to include the ability to exercise consistent and firm discipline, effective communication, and conflict resolution (Campbell 1987). It is argued that the absence of these skills is closely associated with families that are discordant, argumentative and lacking in parental support and supervision (Thomas et al. 1993; Farrington 1994: 11). It is in such families that children are predisposed towards engaging in various antisocial behaviours, including crime and delinquency. It follows, therefore, that if crime is to be prevented, it is necessary for parents to receive training in the skills of care and supervision.

This rendition of the parental failure thesis is based on a narrow understanding of the etiology of crime. It is based on the primary assumption that offending is the end result of certain shortcomings on the caring and supervisory practices of parents. This is not to suggest of course that some parents may indeed be unaware of how to go about supervising and disciplining their children (Utting 1994: 20). However, it is also the case that parenting practices cannot be easily divorced from the material circumstances in which families find themselves, or from the processes by which some families rather than others are subject to state intervention.

The multivariate web

In a prospective longitudinal survey of over 400 traditional working class British boys that began in 1961, family factors were considered alongside a wide range of other predictive indicators (Farrington 1994). The respondents were interviewed over regular periods from the age of 8 to 32 years. The respondents' parents were also interviewed in connection with factors such as income, family size, employment, child rearing practices, and degree of supervision. Teachers were interviewed to establish general patterns of school behaviour among the children, and children's peers were invited to rate factors such as dating, dishonesty, popularity, and troublesomeness.

The study was concerned primarily with the one in five boys who had committed an offense (mainly theft, burglary, taking and driving away of a motor vehicle). No effort was spared by the research team to identify every conceivable relational factor that might be correlated with delinquency. In addition to testing the boys at various chronological stages for intelligence, development, and attainment, the study assessed the impact of living conditions, employment, relationship with parents, leisure activities, and other pursuits such as 'drinking, fighting and offending behaviour' (Farrington 1994: 9).

Faced with such an abundance of factors, the study was able to draw only the most cautious conclusions. Indeed, as Farrington (1994: 14–15) himself observed: '. . . it is difficult to establish which (factor) causes what, or how all these different factors interact to produce delinquency'. Despite such reservations, Farrington was able to outline a number of factors that 'contributed' in one way or another to the onset of delinquency. As mentioned earlier, family factors were particularly important in this regard. According to Farrington (1994: 11) '. . . the presence of adverse family background (poor parental supervision; cruel, passive, or neglecting attitude of the mother; parental conflict) doubled the risk of a later juvenile conviction' . . . We can show that family factors predict delinquency independently of other factors. . . ' (Farrington 1994: 14). For Farrington then, while large family size, low income, poor housing, 'low intelligence', and 'poor school attainment' have a direct bearing on the delinquent behaviour, it is the nature of intrafamily relationships that is most closely associated with antisocial behaviours of young people.

The multivariate approach taken by Farrington to the study of delinquency has been mirrored in a number of other studies in America, New Zealand, and Australia (see Utting et al. 1994 for overview of these studies). Such studies are invariably characterized by the use of vast sample sizes and longitudinal methodologies. Inevitably, this has resulted in the accumulation of a large body of findings that (subject to qualification) may be used to predict the onset of delinquent behaviours. However, the sheer magnitude of the studies, as well as the array of factors under scrutiny, make it difficult to state with absolute certainty which factors are likely to predict which form of delinquency. As another leading figure at the Cambridge Institute of Criminology, David West, points out: 'No survey... can hope to provide a complete map of cause and effect. The most one can expect to do is to identify within an infinitely complex system of interacting influences some items that make a significant contribution to delinquency...' (West 1982: 38).

Perhaps not surprisingly then, survey studies tend to err on the side of caution and the talk is of 'general tendencies' rather than specific 'causes' of delinquency. Having said this, survey studies do focus on particular clusters of factors that are considered to generate delinquency. Yet even in the most sophisticated of multivariate studies, nothing is certain. As Utting, Bright, and Henricson (1994: 11) point out: 'It is important to recognize that statistically significant predictors '... rarely, if ever, approach the realms of certainty'. It has further been noted that: '... attempts to target and stigmatize young children as 'potential offenders' using statistical predictors are likely to misidentify a proportion of children who will not turn to crime, while missing many others who are equally at risk' (Utting 1994: 18). Thus, the exact degree of influence that particular factors engender remains unclear. In short, the causes of offending cannot be specified or generalized to any population of offenders.

Critique

Despite reservations about the ability of empirical research to adequately predict delinquency, it is nonetheless asserted that family dynamics are vital in explaining this phenomenon. In a review of research into families and delinquent behaviour, Junger-Tass (1994: 23) concludes that '... all the research points to the conclusion that internal family dynamics are consistently more important than family structure in affecting delinquency.

Structural factors, such as family disruption, economic dependence, residential mobility and irregular employment of the mother have only a weak effect. They largely have an indirect effect and are mediated by family process variables, such as family control mechanisms and parent-child relationships.' The internal dynamics of the family are thus considered to lie at the heart of delinquent behaviour. This conclusion is repeated with monotonous regularity in countless empirical studies on families and crime—so much so that it is considered axiomatic to any etiological explanation in this area. Such confidence derives from a certainty associated with scientific method through which a systematic process of empirical inquiry allows researchers to produce results and findings. Upon closer examination, however, such confidence turns out to be somewhat less justified than might at first be supposed.

A critical analysis of empirical studies in the area of families and crime must begin by acknowledging the positivist roots of much of the research. The faith placed in scientific method coupled with the failure to theorize connections between such matters as class, power, policing, and deviancy are themselves indicative of a philosophical orientation grounded in individualistic assumptions of human action. Empirical studies in this area are informed by a positivistic approach that emphasizes the role of objective, scientific investigation in seeking to establish the causes of crime and delinquency. Such an approach rests on a set of assumptions about both the role of the investigator in the research process and the subject(s) under study. Specifically, the researcher is considered to occupy a position of scientific detachment or value neutrality allowing him/her to faithfully administer technical methods to the specified area of study. Yet, as Cohen (1974, 1982) points out in relation to British criminological research, the very selection of factors for study mitigates against any simple notion of objectivity. Moreover, positivist researchers fall into the trap of reducing their analyses to single or cluster explanations of social phenomena. Thus, in locating the onset of delinquency in family dynamics, researchers are often prone to abstracting this behaviour from its wider social and economic contexts. Indeed, the emphasis given to the internal dynamics of the family means that such contexts are located in the vague hinterland of the environment.

This form of reductionism results from a largely atheoretical approach to research. The primary business of this sort of research is to identify and predict the particular range of factors that can be correlated with delinquency. Few if any of the studies referred to above attempt to theorize their findings or to deal with awkward methodological issues such as the inherent subjectivity of all social research. Instead, the studies present a series of assertions about the connection between families and crime based upon the security or methodological rigor. Questions associated with the meaning of the family, the relationship between the family and the state and the nature of policing in liberal states are all strenuously avoided or regarded as irrelevant (Hil, McMahon, and Buckley 1996). Moreover, the contested and problematic nature of crime, for example, is rarely acknowledged. The fact that such phenomena are the end result of complex social processes does not seem to concern empirical researchers. The label of offender or delinquent is applied unquestioningly to thousands of young people in an attempt to identify the particular range of factors that differentiate them from the law-abiding majority. This attempt to separate out offenders from the rest of us and record their social attributes is itself symptomatic of a modernist way of thinking about deviance and its origins (Young 1996). It is not too fanciful to argue that the process of researching young people and their families for predictive and classificatory purposes is similar to processes outlined by Foucault in the period of morphological research in the nineteenth century (Foucault 1977). Then, as now, criminologists were intent on identifying the features that distinguished deviants from nondeviants. This in turn underpinned various corrective ideologies that purported to treat offenders so that they could take their rightful place in society (Garland 1994). From Winnicott (1984) and Bowlby onwards, we see prescriptions as to how offending behaviour can be corrected and the role that families should play in this regard. Given the nature of the research informing practice over recent years, it is apparent that such prescriptions are aimed at correcting individual behaviour rather than addressing the need for institutional change.

What is also striking about the empirical research is the way in which it eclipses the voices of subjects. A recent commentary on juvenile justice research noted that the resulting literature is '... remarkable for its lack of attention to the views and experiences of those actually caught up in the criminal justice system. We continue to know little about the lived experience of those involved in processes of criminal justice or about the ways in which these experiences relate to everyday life in communities and neighborhoods' (Hil and McMahon 1995: 4). As if to compound this silence, much of the existing research takes the meaning of the family for granted. In most cases, no effort is made to offer even the most rudimentary definition of this institution. The possibility of alternative family forms and the influence of gender, class, and ethnicity on family relationships are rarely explored in detail. The sole parent household is regarded as deviant to the culturally loaded norm of the complete or intact nuclear family. This narrow view of the family is made worse by the tendency to ignore the diverse and competing interests in family households. Rarely does one get the sense that families are complex, interactive institutions in which power and interest play a significant role in determining relationships therein.

Yet such matters are crucial in enabling us to understand the ways in which family relationships are constructed and acted out in daily life (Funder 1995: 4). The terrible intimacy of family life is reflected in the complex relationships that exist in this ever-changing and culturally diverse social institution (Donaldson 1991:2).

> It is necessary to see families not as unified entities, that can only be represented by the concept of a 'household head', usually male, but as flexible and interactive groupings comprised of men and women, children, young people and older people, whose collective and separate interests need to be protected and supported. (National Council for the International Year of the Family 1994: 9).

Just as it is necessary to remain aware of the complexity of family relationships, so it is important to avoid labeling families as simply 'good' or 'bad'—a polarity implicit in many empirical studies on families and crime. Rather, 'we need an analysis which helps us understand the positive and negative aspects of the family experience for children and young people' (Frost and Stein 1989: 5). By presenting a one-dimensional view of the family, the research tends to buttress oppositional categories that pit one representation of the family against another. Accordingly, families are thought of as normal/abnormal, functional/dysfunctional, broken/complete, and so forth. This rendering of oppositional categories is further underpinned by the assumption that it is possible to demonstrate a quantifiable difference between law-abiding and 'criminogenic' families. This expectation reflects a wider disciplinary discourse that views certain families, communities and neighbours as threats to the social order. Particular households are thus homogenized as problem families and regarded as in need of intervention and regulation (Cook 1997). The process of identifying the particular characteristics of such families through research studies provides the necessary epistemological justification for incursions by the state into the lives of working class families (Parton 1991: 10). The families routinely subject to the most heavy and sustained research and policing are those from the poorest and most disadvantaged sections of the working class (Carrington 1993; Hudson 1993: 3).

While not wishing to suggest a perfect symmetry between academic discourse and institutional practices in respect of families and crime, it is nonetheless evident that research findings have reflected many of the concerns of the state and contributed towards bodies of knowledge that serve to legitimate official intervention. What empirical studies gloss over in their head-long attempt to identify predictive factors are the complex historical and sociopolitical influences bearing down on the family (Donzelot 1979; Devine 1989). To locate crime and delinquency simply in the context of the problematised dysfunctional family is to ignore both the means by which the State seeks to maintain social order and the material conditions that give rise to offending. The failure of empirical studies to articulate a cogent understanding of relations between families and the wider social world has produced a view of the family that is both abstract and ahistorical. This is compounded by a number of sweeping pronouncements on the moral character of families. Thus, criminogenic families are said to be more discordant, conflictual, or argumentative than other more law-abiding households. Such families are also contrasted with the idealistic functional and intact household. The use of these glib terms has served to obscure the lived realities of working class life and to regard crime as the simple by-product of the failing family (Hil and McMahon 1995; Cook 1997). As Mike Donaldson (1991: 2) points out, an understanding of working class families must draw on 'the whole lives of its members, changing and changed by each other as they stand in structural opposition to capital, its forces and agencies.'

The daily life of the family-household is acted out in a multiplicity of ways according to the essential divisions of age and gender (Donaldson 1991: 73). The 'struggle to create order and meaning out of precariousness and scarcity, to provide a measure of security in a very uncertain world,' involves managing various household clocks (Donaldson 1991: 73). The organization of family time and relationships between members is, however, severely disrupted by problems associated with unemployment and poverty. At such times, families strive to manage increasingly fraught and fragile relationships (Altatt and Yeandle 1992: 144). For those on the margins of economic life—the long term unemployed, the chronically poor, the isolated and disaffected—the family household becomes less a source of respite and support and more a place in which the pressures of the outside world are acted out. The recent tendency of governments to devolve greater social and economic responsibility has simply added to many of the pressures already faced by working class families (Hartley and Woolcott 1994). To simply ignore such matters, or to relegate them to the status of background factors, as do many of the studies on families and crime, is to deny the role of external forces in shaping intimate relationships (Holman 1995).

Conclusion

Over the past few decades the proliferation of research into families and crime has yielded a rich harvest of results and findings. Particular attention has been paid to factors such as the broken home, family size, lack of parental supervision, poor child rearing skills and lack of parental warmth and love. Although almost every aspect of family life appears to have been scrutinized in the search for the ultimate causes of crime, there is little agreement about which specific factors lead to delinquency. In the most researched area of all, broken families, the connection with delinquency is described variously as weak or not at all strong. Perhaps the strongest conclusion to emerge from these studies is that inconsistent discipline and lack of warmth and love (particularly on the mother's side) can be linked with antisocial behaviour. Even here, however, studies are limited by their failure to define such nebulous terms as love and warmth. Indeed, it is arguable that many of the researchers' observations may be based on highly subjective (and culturally loaded) interpretations of family functioning. For example, the labeling of a family as 'argumentative' or 'conflictual' may not accord with the views of family members themselves. Moreover, family conflict may in fact constitute one part of a complex web of relations within the family. How, for example, does one pit conflict against loyalty and a sense of belonging in the overall schema of family life? Research studies have tended to focus on atomized features of family life, and they have often done so to the exclusion of any theoretical understanding of the position of the family in the wider social world. The family is thus rendered abstract and atheoretical. In failing to address the way in which crime and delinquency is socially constructed empirical studies fall into the modernist trap of regarding offenders and their families as fundamentally different to the rest of us. Finally, in the feverish pursuit of predictive indicators it appears that empirical researchers have largely glossed over the ways in which subjects themselves talk about their experiences. Indeed, it is striking how little we know of what family members have to say about the effects of juvenile crime on them. It is to this neglected field that we now turn.

Chapter Five

The Watts Family: A Case Study

An unintended outcome of much qualitative research is that, while the voices of those involved are heard, they are heard in fragmented and disjointed ways. Often, this is because the material is analyzed according to subjects and themes that virtually determine that people's conversations are cut and pasted into grab-bites of significance for the overall effect of the research. It is not often that those researched are able to have an extended playing of their conversations with the researcher. This chapter will allow the voices of one of the families in this study to be heard in more detail than is common in studies like this.

The Watts family was interviewed over a 20-month period. There were four interviews altogether, three with the mother, Susan, and the stepfather, Chris, and one with Anne Boyd, John's grandmother and the mother of Susan Watts. John Watts took part in the interview with his grandmother with whom he was staying at the time. As if to prefigure their criticisms of childless child welfare workers, Susan and Chris Watts insisted that the person who interviewed them be a parent. At the end of the first interview with them, Anthony McMahon noted, 'I felt a bit depressed after talking to them. They seemed to have done lots of things to make John more responsible but nothing seems to have worked. I felt that their kid could have been mine and that's what made me depressed I guess ... As I was leaving, Susan said "what's the next stage (with John)?" She said it as if she expected me to know; that's a bit of a worry because I'm sure I don't know' (Field notes, February 17, 1996).

The family

Susan and Chris Watts live in a high-set wooden house, typical of housing in North Queensland. The front room of the house runs the width of the building. It is sparsely furnished with couches, chairs and a thin, light-brown carpet. A long, narrow hall runs to the back of the house with rooms off each side. The first room on the right is the kitchen. The hallway floor is covered and spotted with dried paint from a seemingly enthusiastic painting job. In the backyard there is a salt water swimming pool with a small spa at the end nearer the house. Next to the pool is a shaded area and behind that a trampoline.

Susan Watts is a plump woman in her late thirties. She is a white Australian of Irish/Scottish extraction and has a job as a sales assistant. Chris Watts is about six feet tall, heavy set with dark hair, also in his late thirties. He, too, is a white Australian and is of Welsh/English descent. He had had his own business, which had taken up all his time for five years, but he had to wind down the business. At the time of the first interview he was unemployed but found work soon after. He seems very definite about things and tends to believe his word is law. Their son, John, had just turned 15 years old when the Watts were first interviewed and was not living with his parents but with his grandmother in another part of town. A younger brother, Paul, aged six years, lived with his parents. When the final interview with the parents was made 20 months after the first interview, John was in a juvenile detention facility.

Susan spoke about her son:

> He's really funny. When we're doing things together like painting, or gardening, or something, he comes out with the funniest things, but he doesn't seem to have any drive or motivation to get himself anywhere. He will rely on everybody else because we've always been picking the pieces up... He tells so many lies that you just don't know what to believe and it is really hard to trust him very much. We don't know whether to believe him or not. As a child he was very truthful; now he's absolutely done a complete flip. When he was in primary school, some of the little kids from the school he was going to used to come in and see me at work and I was a bit of a celebrity because I was John Watts's mum: 'Hey, mum, it's John Watts's mum.' It was like that. But he's no role model.

Chris added:

I put it down to a backlash because when he was a little kid before Susan and I got married, he was the only one for everybody to dote over. Before he came to live at my place he never even ate his meals at the kitchen table, it was all in front of the television. Coming here was a little bit of a culture shock for him because he ate all of his meals at the table. After Paul arrived he wasn't an only child, and like, especially when Paul was a baby, Susan had to give all her attention to the baby all the time because they demand so much. John virtually had the best of everything and he thinks he deserves the best of everything. I really feel that he wants the best of everything, so he's done his best to try and get it for himself.

Susan:

But there is little effort on his part.

John's offending

When did he first start offending?

Chris:

Well, the first one that we actually knew about was when John was just 13 and he and a friend of his jumped a fence and stole tee-shirts off a clothes line and we found out that he actually had some offending before that. But, everything was very minor; like we found that he was going around pinching things out of open windows. Or, you know, a kid left his roller blades beside a tree so John went along and pinched them and the kid had a watch with it, and he grabbed that as well. Everything was virtually minor straight off. Then, he met these kids at a shelter for street kids and these kids told him how to hot wire a car and that sort of thing. That is when he started to try and break into cars; he actually had tried breaking into cars, but he couldn't get them started before. He went on from there to stealing cars but he only really wanted to take the cars on a joy ride. Then it came to break and entry into motels and that sort of thing, where he was able to get the night's takings or something like that because he seemed to be, you know, collecting two or three hundred dollars at a time.

Susan:

(When John was) in Grade 8 (the first year of High School), we had to go to Sydney for three nights and we'd arranged for Paul to go to my girlfriend's place and John went to his friends who also went to the same High School. We called John every day, actually, and John was telling us the story of how his friend had his bike stolen by this kid from another suburb and how they went over there before school and stole the bike back. John took great delight in telling us how they did all this detective work to find the kid. When we got back from Sydney, we went down to my girlfriend's house to pick him up and she said, 'Oh, he's gone down to your place, he had to meet his aunt.' Subsequently, we discovered that the two of them had been wagging school (truanting) while we were gone and when we came back here the plot started to unfold. We found out that he wasn't even going to school at that time. From what we understand, instead of going off to school, they'd come here for a little while, and then they'd go around to somebody else's place and because there are kids around here that wag school and because both parents work, or single parents work, they've got fridges that they can raid all over the place and so if a kid wanted to run away from home for several weeks, he could get fed every day very easily. And before we got home, John borrowed money from some of his friends and sold his shoes and stuff to get the money to catch the bus to Cairns because he knew he would be in trouble. And then the police rang us and said, 'We've picked your son up. He's in Cairns. Can you drive up and pick him up?' So we spent four and a half hours driving to Cairns at 11 o'clock at night. So we didn't get home again until 8:30 the next morning. And that was after a day of traveling from Sydney to Townsville.

What did you say to him at that particular instance?

Chris:

The situation basically was that he wanted to be able to come and go as he liked. Even go around to kid's places at 10:30 at night and we stressed to him, like we took examples of children who were friends of his who were in trouble and who were not and virtually, by naming them and saying, 'Well, is this kid allowed out at night' and he'd say, 'Yes' and I would say, 'Is he known by the police?' 'Yes.' 'Okay, what about this kid here? Is he allowed out at night?' 'No' 'Has he ever been in trouble with the police? 'No.' And we stressed to him that parents who knew where their kids were all the time, had no problems with their children. But we knew for a fact that he used to sneak out of our place at one o'clock in the morning, or as soon as we went to sleep, and go off for hours because I'd go up and check his bed and if he wasn't in it, I'd sit on it and wait until he got home.

John left home a number of times after this. He usually stayed with friends and, as Susan says, 'there was a lot of drugs and stuff involved.' Once he stayed at his aunt's place for two weeks but she found it too stressful to have him.

The Watts Family: A Case Study

Susan:

> So we brought him back here and within three days (of him returning) we went to a friend's place for pizza and he didn't wish to come. We said, 'Okay, you can stay home.' We were gone for three hours and on returning nothing was said. But the next morning he said, 'I've got to go and see a friend and get some bike parts.' Well, he rang me that afternoon at work and said, 'I'm ringing you because I have to, because last night I took Chris's car for a drive and I got picked up by the police and the policeman said I had to ring you or else they were going to ring.' And I said, 'Don't you think that was not a sensible thing to do.' And he didn't come home that night and hitchhiked to Ingham because he then rang from Ingham after that and he needed money and I said: 'No, I'm sorry, this is your choice.'
>
> He eventually came back. He said he rolled some man in a park and got his wallet, or something. So he bought Chris a present which was supposed to make up for stealing his car and half his coin collection and thought he would just cruise back in. So my sister picked him up from the bus and took him to her place. At which time, through Family Services, we'd arranged for him to stay at a street kids shelter. He went out there and he was there for three weeks and then he got expelled from there for growing marijuana on their property. And the night that he was expelled, they (staff at the shelter) refused to drive him anywhere and they told me not to go and pick him up. We just let him go and make his own way. He did ring me twice that night because we've got an answering machine. Then I was quite annoyed with my mother at the time because the next day he contacted her and wanted someone else to pick up the pieces, you know.

John, then, based himself more or less at his grandmother's house.

Chris:

> John moved out of our home when he would have been about 13 And it was virtually a situation where he was living with his grandmother and we were sending him to a boarding school, but he didn't like it there. So he got himself kicked out of the boarding school. And, you know, we virtually gave him an ultimatum and said, you know, like, you've got a home here, but you've got to live by what our rules are. Our rules are just the same as for any other 13-year-old kid that you know. But he wanted to be able to come and go as he pleased. And that didn't really fit in with what we wanted. And, he talked his grandmother into staying there. And you know, she had no control over him.

Parents' responses

What was your response when you first found out he had been arrested for stealing?

Chris:
> It was probably one of disbelief in one way because we thought he had so much potential, because he's quite a smart kid. But, you know, the thing with drugs hurts most because he promised us he'd never bring drugs into the house. And we found drugs in his room. We found places around the house where he'd planted marijuana, and the thing that made us really, really angry was the fact that he would tell us that he'd turned over a new leaf. We felt he had—our word then was he just turned around and shit on us, sort of thing. Yeah.
>
> We didn't think he was on drugs at all at first. We just thought that, you know, he was just going through a difficult time. But, you know, the drugs explained a lot, too. Like, for example, if there was something going on like a party down the road and we told him that he couldn't go, it didn't matter. Like, he'd sneak out when we were asleep and he really couldn't care that we knew that he'd gone. But, you know, that really brought out a lot of anger when he said he wasn't on drugs and then we found drugs here or he'd promise that he'd never bring drugs home and he'd actually planted them downstairs.

Susan:
> We'd be weeding the garden and finding pot plants hidden away and also on top of his air conditioner in his bedroom and in his closet and you'd go 'Argh!' And he even went so far as to say, 'Oh, no, you just leave them there, it'll be okay with the police. I'll tell them they're my own plants and you had nothing to do with it.' I mean, I'm not falling for that one. I said, 'It doesn't matter, John, You just can't have them here.' John had also got himself into a crowd that were selling prescription drugs. A girl he knew had them for pain and she didn't use it all so she used to go around and sort of doctor shop and get all these drugs and then she'd sell them to all the kids.

Chris:
> We had many long discussions with John about the people he was hanging around with and getting into trouble with. Because he knew it was wrong and each time he told us he wouldn't do it again. We've done a lot of work for John as far as all the worrying and all the running around we've done. All the chasing up of him by ringing up parents of his known friends and asking them if they've seen him. Running to this corner and that corner because someone has sighted him. We were virtually told to get on with our own lives.

The Watts Family: A Case Study

Susan:

I mean, we've spent weeks of not knowing where he was. And we've had the house staked out from the inside with all the windows and doors locked, waiting for him to come home because he'd been on the run. We've spent hours driving the streets and we found him once at a skating rink and Chris took off after him, chasing him through the neighbourhood, while I was waiting for the police to arrive. We have just spent like two years from hell. It's just been unbelievable, especially when we didn't know where he was.

What did he say to you about his offending?

Chris:

John used all these different reasons and you don't know what to believe and what not to believe. We spoke to him one time when we thought that he had settled down and now realized that what he did before was wrong. We asked him what his side of the story would be and he said, 'Well, if it makes any difference, I think, like, if I was in your position I would have changed for the child.'

Susan:

That's what he said, 'I would have changed for the child.' And 'I think you should allow me to grow my own personal marijuana here.' I just said to him, 'You have got to be joking.' I said, 'I'm sorry; but this is our home. Marijuana is illegal and you're not growing it in my garden.' I mean, I have pulled lots of it out. And he used to grow it in his wardrobe and on top of his air-conditioner and stuff like this. But he seemed to think that I was really unreasonable for not allowing him to grow his own personal marijuana.

So what was your reaction when all of this was happening, Susan?

Susan:

It was just like shock, you know. This stuff can't be happening. I didn't believe it and I didn't know what was the matter and there was nothing that we could do to change anything. It seemed like there was nowhere really to go either. Later on, I think it was a little later, maybe the following year after he'd been expelled from another school, we then asked Family Services for some help and was given a slim amount. We asked for counseling and they said counseling was available and gave us a name. However, they said to us and to John, that it would only be with John's consent that he went to counseling. But they put it in such a way that John just said to me, 'Oh, it's OK, Mum, I can sort myself out. I don't need that sort of stuff.' You know, if it had been put across maybe a little differently, that might have been much more of a help. But it was just disgusting.

So what sort of effect did it have on the family?

Chris:

Well, we nearly got divorced.

Susan:

Oh, it seemed that every argument we had was always about John. And it was just ripping us apart. And we've got another young fellow (their son, Paul), and although you try not to say anything in front of the children, I feel that it upset him, too.

Chris:

Well, Paul has got behavioural problems ... we do know that Paul did have a few behavioural problems by the shenanigans that John had been up to.

Susan:

And Paul actually says to me, 'Why isn't John here?' and 'He should be with his family.' And I say, 'Well, grandma needs him to do jobs.' He says to his brother, 'John, you don't have to work anymore, you can come home with us.'

Police, social workers, and courts

The Wattses felt isolated in the court and juvenile justice systems. A further feeling of isolation arose from the lack of support services available to parents. They were critical of police, social workers, and the courts because of the narrow focus of the services offered. Services were not seen to meet the needs they had as parents.

What advice did people give you about John?

Chris:

We were virtually told to wait until he hits rock bottom and then handle it as though we were always there for him, but we weren't to be running around the streets wrecking our own lives for him either.

This has been going on since he was about thirteen. Realistically, there's no one out there, like when I was a teenager, the police used to make kids go to school. Now they don't. They don't want to know about kids. And the teachers don't care, you know. As far as they're concerned, if that kid's not a model child they're quite happy for him

The Watts Family: A Case Study

not to be there because then he's not disturbing the rest of the children in the class. So, it's a no-win situation for the parents. I honestly believe that the government's really got to work out what can be done here, and realistically I believe that the whole police service needs to have a shake up.

Tell me about the first time you had to go to the police station.

Chris:

Well, the first time when we got a phone call to say that he's down at the police station, we did the parental thing of going down there and it was me who got interviewed by the sergeant. Now, John had been at the police station for more than two hours. And every time one of the policemen walked past him, he said, 'Son, we're going to get you for this. You've overstepped the line.' Every policeman who walked past was ribbing him each time. And when I turned up, there was no more of that. We walked straight into the sergeant's office and he said to John, 'Listen, son, do you know the difference between right and wrong?' To which he said, 'Yes.' And the sergeant said, 'Well, you're not going to do this again, are you?' And John said, 'No.' And he said, 'Well, let's hope we don't see you again.' And that was the end of it.

He told all of his friends about that. Like, whereas I believe they should have come down on him stronger from the start. So he treated it as a joke. It was just a good thing for him to show off to his friends what he could do.

Susan:

I've been to court with him heaps of times, and it's a social affair. This juvenile court cracks me up. They (the offenders) all stand outside and laugh and joke and then they go inside and then it's even bigger jokes when they come out and they only got a warning. And the Judge says to them each and every time when they give these warnings to them, 'Next time you're going to go.' And next time they don't. It's okay to be lenient, and if you're going to be lenient, fine. But don't say something totally different to the kids. They think it's a big joke.

What were your initial contacts with Family Services?

Chris:

Everything was polite. Probably one of our initial contacts we had with Family Services was on behalf of John because he wanted Living Away From Home Allowance (a Federal Government allowance for young people who cannot live at home) saying that he couldn't live with me because I used to hit him. I honestly believe that he was put up to it by his friends for him to try and get the Living Away From

Home Allowance. Well, I demonstrated to (Family Services) how I used to get frustrated and give him a clip over the ear. I told them that my father used to hit me with my Scout belt. Also we had a feather duster which had a cane handle; I used to get belted with that.

I never saw anything wrong with giving him a clip over the ear. You know, they (Family Services) didn't really give us any guidance whatsoever on what you're supposed to do and they never took any action. But they come around and my way of thinking was that they put their beak in. And they weren't a help to me and they weren't a help to Susan or John, really. They just virtually assessed the situation as to say that the child wasn't in danger. They never really gave us any ideas on which way we should head. As they got to know us a bit more when John was under supervision with them and Susan used to go in there a fair bit as well; they were a bit more of a help then. But initially they just use words like, 'If you don't think you want to cooperate with us, you know, we can use stronger measures.' You know, speaking firmly (to us) but not really giving us any answers.

Anyway, we went and fronted up to the Family Services on a couple of occasions for that purpose, and on another couple of occasions for interviews regarding his supervision which has to be reviewed every now and again. We had gotten to know the people at Family Services at that time and they had virtually given us an assurance that we weren't bad parents. Whenever they wanted to see us or whatever, we would be there, we would be on time, we'd be prompt. Whereas, on John's part, he wouldn't turn up half the time and they seem to be writing reports in our favour at that time.

Are there things that Family Services or police or the courts could do that would be of assistance to families like yourself?

Chris:

The thing that got to me there was that they had their job from nine till five, that was it. They've done their duty.

Susan:

There was no offer to help or to ask 'what can we do for you?' Once John finished his stint of probation it was, 'Goody, we have one off our books.'

So you're saying that they didn't see you as a family?

Susan:

No. They just had to investigate any complaint that is made. Which is fair enough. That's their job. But they know our family. They know our son. They know that we went in their looking for help and didn't get any. Surely, there should be another branch of Family Services that can help families with juvenile offenders to work through some sort of strategy. Even if it's just a little group. But just propping up the courts is all they're doing. Their job is to make sure they sign the book once a week.

Well, is there anything that you think could be done to assist parents in court?

Susan:

The courts only do anything to assist parents when it gets to the 'no return' status. When (the court) will put him under a Care and Protection Order and we'll pick him up and take him to school every day and make sure that he's there and bring him home. I think they call that Care and Protection which is another Family Services role. But that's really a long way down the track. And if they had done something like that a little bit earlier, there's a possibility that they would be able to redeem these kids. But they have laws, rules that they have to follow and those laws and rules aren't allowing them to do things properly. When it's too late, what's the point?

Chris:

Realistically, the police don't even want to know anything about kids.

Susan:

Because it's a total waste of their time. They know perfectly well, they take them in there and then they're out. Why would they bother? What they're doing now is not working. What they're doing is actually making it worse. I was actually fortunate enough to go to school in Brisbane where a lot of kids were from this outcare home, which was a Salvation Army Home, and those kids were put in there, not because they were repeat offenders, but because they couldn't get along with their parents at home.

Has John had contact with alcohol and drugs services at all?

Susan:

Ha, it was a joke. We wanted him to have alcohol and drug counseling and we spoke to the Family Services, who arranged the visit with the Drug Rehabilitation. John went along there maybe twice or three times. But John just went there because the guy knew so much about drugs. Mate, he was going along there, it was like school, you know, almost taking notes.

Parents' responsibility

Do you think that parents should be asked to go to court and take responsibility for the offenses of children?

Chris:
> I think they should in some ways there, yeah. But I also feel that, in some situations parents aren't allowed to control their children neither. In our situation, we virtually had visits from family services and that sort of thing when I was bodily holding John back from going out and roaming the streets at night. I think a lot of people would be of the view to say, 'Oh, yeah, those parents must be not doing the right thing and so they should be made to pay for those children's crimes,' because they would be thinking about what happens to the victim. But the kid just gets off Scot free on most occasions.

Susan:
> Except I feel sorry for the parents of those children. They're then victimized by society.

How would you answer those who say that parents are responsible for their children's behaviour?

Chris:
> Well, you just can't judge every book by one cover. I've thought about this long and hard over several years really because I understand the situation, but you can't really always blame the parents for what the children do. Like, one family John was hanging around, the mother had given up. She had seven kids ranging from the ages of four to 17, and she couldn't control those kids. All that she was doing was providing a home for them. She was working, she wasn't collecting unmarried mother's benefits and that sort of thing. She had really given up but you wouldn't be able to make her pay back any money because she wouldn't have been earning enough to pay anything back.
>
> You know, you really have to judge every situation as it is. For example, if a parent doesn't care where their kids are, because that's what all this bloody comes back to, because everybody says, 'Oh, look at that parent, doesn't care where the kids are,' I believe that if that's true, well, the parent is at fault. But if it comes to the situation where your child is just walking out and saying, 'Oh, look, I'm not going to stay here. I'm just going to walk out. I want to be with my friends'—which is what happened to us—you really are trying. I really believe that my opinion changed when I was put in that

position myself, so I honestly feel that you can't really judge a book by its cover.

But, you know, there are some parents out there who don't really care where their children are, especially those ones who it's like often in the Casino and leave the kids in the car, that sort of thing, that's not right. But, you know, we were ringing Family Services to see if they could help us. So, I'm certainly of the opinion that we aren't responsible for his actions, that's for sure. The people that reckon that you should be able to know where your kids are every day of the week are right, you should do. But if you've got a child who is a runaway kid, you don't. Once the kid is out of your care and control, there is nothing much you can do. You can't control a kid 24 hours a day. You can't keep him wrapped up in cotton wool.

Susan:

We can't control him full stop. He's at the age where he's in control of his own life. Well, I think that there are cases when it is the parents' fault. But there are many, many varied cases where it might be a combination or where it might not have nothing to do with the parents. You cannot pinpoint anything specific because each person is an individual and there is so many different and varied things that tip them over: Drugs, alcohol, family. You know, it could be anything. So they can't just say 'the family.'

What advice would you, as parents, give to other parents who are in similar situations?

Susan

That we don't have any answers. I mean . . .

Chris (interrupting):

Well, one of the things that Susan and I really fell down as a team was that Susan was the soft one. John knew that he could badger his mother, even if it took half an hour, three-quarters of an hour, or two hours, he knew that he could push his mother over. He could get by. Whereas, with me I would stick to my guns. If I said 'no,' he couldn't do it, well, I'd made my decision. That's probably the reason for the bit of a fall out that he had with me, but unfortunately, I'm not going to change too much from that within reason. We always let him have plenty of time to state his side of the story as well. So we've always wanted to be clear on both sides, but the other thing is, too, which I feel was a big factor, was Paul coming into vogue, John wasn't the only one getting all the attention either.

Susan:
> Yes. The other thing was that we should have maybe have done more as a family earlier on when he was a willing participant. We did lots of things, but I think we could have done more.

Are you saying you blame yourselves?

Chris:
> We don't think that we're blameless, that's for sure. We feel that there's got to be some blame rested upon ourselves. I really feel that the only answer to beat his ideas was to show to him that he had a home where he knew where he stood, and he just couldn't get away with things. Whereas he feels that he could tell us anything and he'd just tell us what we wanted to hear, and go and do whatever he liked. But the other thing is the drug side of it. I don't ever believe that there is a way you can get around that. And as far as I'm concerned, the cops are gutless wonders because they know the kids who are dealing drugs at schools and they're not doing anything about it. If you spoke to most parents and found that someone was dealing drugs to their kids, they'd be ropeable. These police just think it's everyday life now.
>
> We sat down with John for hours and hours at this table, and there was no way that we could actually get into his head that what he was doing was wrong. He was only living life for the next five minutes and he couldn't see any further. Communication is the main thing. There's no other thing for it; communicate so that you can understand each other.

Susan, what do you think is going to happen in the future?

Susan:
> With John, I have no idea. I know what I'd like to see, but I don't know if that's going to happen because he's become too lazy. His get up and go has got up and went. So I would just love him to finish Year 12 and then get a job or go to University. I've tried to tell him how much fun they have at university and this sort of thing.

Do you think he'll grow out of this offending?

Susan:
> Oh, I'm almost positive he will. It's not as if it's the family business and so the people around him don't do that sort of thing. So he really will grow, mature a bit and see that this is just not normal. One would hope. He keeps talking about going in and getting himself a job, and I think to myself, I would prefer him to go to school. But that's up to

him. He's been quite cooperative; chatty. It's like nothing has ever happened and he's our best friend, if you know what I mean.

Twenty months later

What's John doing now?

Chris:

A couple of months ago, he went for a little trip down to Mackay and broke into a few places down there and the police caught him there and since then he's been in police custody and he's at Cleveland now. So we know he's not in jail—we know he's not in trouble at present because he's in custody.

Susan:

Around that time I had been speaking with him possibly once a week but it was very rare that you could actually find him home because he would go out and not return for days on end and my mother would have no idea where he was. From that time and even till now, his only friends seem to have been his co-offenders which is why each time he comes out of Cleveland, they're the only people that he knows. So he just slips straight back into it. He has a real difficulty handling his alcohol, so all he has to do is start up a bit of alcohol and have a couple of marijuana joints and he's away. And he says that he loses control of things and he has no idea of what he's doing half the time, and that's very scary insofar as his latest rash of break and enters. He sort of went down to Mackay for a weekend with no intention to do anything wrong. He had money in his pocket. But he committed ten break and enters in one or two days. And that's what he's back in jail for now. He's good in Cleveland and he's really rushing to get through his Year 10 (sophomore year) because he wants to have that finished before he comes out; he's due to come out in February. In February he's going to turn 17 and realizes that he's going to have to go to Stuart Prison if he continues. That's been his plan all along, I think. It's like you can offend all the way up until you're 17 but you shouldn't do it after you're 17. Somehow he thinks that when you turn 17 you'll just magically stop. But you get to 17 and you don't have any other friends. So what do you do?

What kind of impact does John's recent offending have on you now?

Susan:

Oh, insofar as our family life, we don't really let it interfere with it any longer. We don't let it worry us any more. Basically, John's living away, if he's not in Cleveland, he's living with his grandmother and other places. I go and see him (in Cleveland) once a week and my mum goes and sees him once a week. When he went in there this time everybody was so angry with him that we left him there for a while without going and seeing him.

Chris:

Well, I've stepped aside at present. It's the sort of situation where I just feel that if I can be listened to by John and by Susan and by John's grandmother I would have an input. But I don't believe I'd be listened to. So , . . .

Susan:

No, Chris doesn't have anything to do with John at all.

What would you say to John if he was listening to you?

Chris:

Oh, basically, that he has to set goals and he's got to achieve those goals. The other thing I'd talk to him about is that he should never, ever drink so much alcohol or get into drugs where he just hasn't got control over himself. If he's going to get violent where he's smashing things up, what would happen if a security car came along and he belted that security guard on the head with a piece of iron and killed him? What do you say, that I was just so drunk that I didn't know what I was doing?

How are you feeling about John at the moment?

Susan:

Oh, I'm OK. He's in custody and while he's in custody he does the right thing. If he doesn't the guys down there deal with him and they put him in the time-out room where he's locked up. He's there till February. He was given nine months. His sentence should have been apparently a lot longer, but the judge felt sorry for him and gave him a shorter sentence. And last week we went to court again, and the week before we went to court as well, and they were for the same offenses. There was two hang-over ones from Mackay. They were the drug offenses where he was caught with possessing some drugs and also supply. The supply was to some kid at some shelter with some marijuana or something.

Every time he goes into Cleveland and dries out I think, 'Yes, this'll be it.' But then again, you can't give up hope for them. He's currently doing the right thing insofar as he's doing his Year 10 (sophomore year) and he's hoping to have that finished, totally done by the time he leaves in February. He's done a First Aid certificate and he was so proud of himself. But then I will just wait and see and as Christopher says, 'It's not what he says, it's what he does.' So we just have to wait and see what he does.

So what are your aspirations for him now?

Susan:

What I would like to see is that when he comes out that he really needs to find some new friends and maybe get involved in something that doesn't involve breaking into houses and stuff.

Chris, what are your aspirations for John?

Chris:

I just go back to my famous quotes where I say, 'It's not what he says he's going to do, it's what he's going to do.'

Conclusion

John's offending has had far-reaching consequences for his family. His parents' emotions went from shock to dismay, anger, frustration, and resignation. Their story certainly questions the popular assumption that parents are indifferent to the offending behaviours of their children. Rather than simply abdicating their supervisory duties, John's parents (and grandmother) were actively involved in efforts to deal with and put a stop to his offending. They supported him when he went to court and visited him when he was in prison. They have not abandoned him, although they are the first to admit they don't know what else to do.

Susan and Chris Wattses' impotence to counter their son's offending is further compounded by their perception of the impotence, or irrelevance, of the interventions of the police, welfare workers, and court officials. They seem to provide their harshest criticisms at these workers rather than direct them at their son. Their biggest disappointment about the workers involved with their son is that he is the focus of attention and not themselves as a family. They show a real anger and puzzlement at what they see as an undermining of their roles as parents.

This chapter has been one family's story of juvenile offending. The next chapter will distill the experience of the 20 families interviewed for this study. Many of them will echo the experiences of the Watts' family; many, though, have different stories to tell.

CHAPTER SIX

Parents' Experiences of Juvenile Offending

This chapter considers parents' responses to the initial realization of their child's offending and parents speak about the ways in which they reacted to it. Their stories contradict the prevalent belief that the parents of juvenile offenders do not care about the offending of their children.

Most of the interviews with the parents were conducted while the children were continuing to offend. This meant that the parents were still coming to terms with having a juvenile offender in the family. Some were still angry, while others had progressed to some sort of resignation. Very few had had the luxury of calm reflection on the offending careers of their children.

Finding out about offending

Of the 20 families interviewed for this study, 19 parents said they responded with embarrassment, self-doubt, shame, and anger to the knowledge of their child's offending. Parents described a mixture of extreme and conflicting emotions when first told of their child's offending. The bad news was often relayed by a third party and, in many cases, by the police. One parent said that she was told by a relative, 'Oh . . . Family Services was looking for you,' some days after her son was arrested.

The common theme in reactions to offending was the understandable range of emotions expressed by parents on learning of their children's criminal activities. Parents revealed an overwhelming sense of frustration and a desire to understand the reasons for their child's behaviour. This appeared to be due in part to coming to terms with the offending; however, the offending ultimately served to reinforce the view that they had failed as parents.

Speaking about her first realization of her son Tim's offending, Brenda Jones said,

> I found it very hard to accept, especially with the issue of drugs (marijuana). I can't really understand why kids feel the need to take drugs, so I had great difficulty coming to terms with it. I felt upset; angry with him for putting me through it; helpless because he didn't particularly seem to want any help; very angry that the police were involved because I'm not used to dealing with that type of thing. It's very hard.
>
> I asked all the usual questions, 'Why? How could you have been so stupid?' And I just got the usual pack of lies that it wasn't his fault, he'd never do it again (which he did; he hasn't stopped, actually).
>
> I think my main reactions were stress, helplessness, depression to a certain extent, aloneness, a terrible, terrible aloneness. There's nobody you can turn to that's going to say, 'Look, it's okay. It's okay to be feeling like this. You don't have to feel like that. This kid is at fault, not you.' If just one official person had said that, I think you could probably handle it a little bit better.
>
> It's very difficult because each time I tried to talk about it, I just got abused. He'd throw a tantrum and start calling me names. He'd walk out of the house. He'd disappear. He wasn't particularly interested in talking about it. He got his official warning (from the Children's Court); they didn't charge him. They just gave him an official warning. And he got out of there and he said, 'Oh, well, I'm fine now, I've got away with it.' And that was it (Brenda Jones, mother of Tim, aged 17).

Mary Smith was angry when she found out her son, Peter, also aged 17, was stealing in order to buy marijuana: 'I was very angry with him. I just didn't understand why he was doing these things.'

> He's always been very rebellious, though. He's never had a very good attitude towards school authority. I became aware that he was going to other kids' houses when he wasn't at school, mostly on weekends, on holidays and doing things they weren't supposed to be doing, like stealing, breaking and entering and stealing things and bringing them home. He was also taking things out of our house without our knowledge, you know, CDs and small electrical appliances, even his own stereo equipment, and pawning them. He was taking money out of my husband's wallet and my purse all the time and even when we had visitors he would take money from them, including my own family, my sister. (It was) a nightmare, yes, very worrying because he

has lots of good in him, you know, and it was hard seeing him just going downhill.

Wendy Reynolds, the mother of 12-year-old Lester, has four children from two marriages. Her current husband is not the father of her children. Lester is her second child and the one in trouble. His offending makes her feel 'inadequate, not doing the job properly, not being a parent. You blame yourself a lot. You just think that you could have been a better parent, that you maybe should have done things differently, that circumstances in your life should have been handled differently.'

> When I first moved up here (Townsville), which was seven years ago, that was basically really when he started getting into a lot of trouble because he was only four when I moved up here. So he wasn't really in a lot of trouble then, he was just a difficult little child. So it's only been since I've been with Sam (her husband) that he's had all this trouble.
>
> (When I first had children), I had no idea what parenting was. Absolutely none, but I thought it would come natural over the years, that you would grow and develop with them and it would all fall into place and I would have two boys, two girls, a nice little family where they'd all go off and finish school. I thought it was just going to happen. I just wanted my children to finish school, stay out of trouble, and be happy. Boy have I been let down . . . I cried an awful lot. I still do occasionally (Wendy Reynolds).

Ingrid Perkins is the mother of Robert, aged 15. Mrs Perkins has five children. Robert, who is her youngest child, two grandchildren and a niece were living with her at the time of the interview. The Perkins are an Aboriginal family who have lived around Townsville for many years. The four older children grew up with their father and only occasionally visit their mother. Robert briefly got into trouble when he was eight years old for stealing money. However, when he turned 13, he began to steal cars and break into houses to steal. Mrs Perkins explained her feelings on first hearing of his offenses.

> Oh, I was very upset at the time because I didn't know what to expect. It was just a first offense. He was mixing with some other kids at the time and I didn't know much about these other kids, but, you know, I can't blame anybody but himself and myself, I suppose. I don't know, I just felt a bit, you know, a bit hurt at the time. Yeah.

And when it started happening again then, you know, it was just like it kept going on and on; the policemen always coming past shining the light at my house and that. They was checking up on him. Yeah. I just used to get that fear in me all the time, you know, of them (police), too. You know, I just was afraid. I didn't know what to do. You know, it was sort of hard growing up a child on my own, you know, growing him up. Yeah, because the other children were grown up with their father, you see.

I just felt like I couldn't talk to anybody really. I was thinking, oh, it was all my fault, you know. I sort of took all the blame what was happening to him. So no one couldn't help me unless I helped myself. I had to do something for myself. So I didn't really turn to anybody. Family Services said they would come around and take him away for jobs when he was out on good behaviour, but I never really talked to anybody about it. I didn't want anybody to know about what was happening in my life and in our lives. It was no one else's business. Yeah. And I just felt that I had to sort it out myself. I don't know, I feel that sometimes maybe I'm the one whose supposed to do all this and I can't put blame on anybody else. I don't know what to do, really, sometimes. I just got to leave it all and I don't know, let it go by, let it happen itself. I don't know what to do (Ingrid Perkins).

Helen Joyce is the mother of Amy, aged 13. The Joyce family are Aboriginal. Helen Joyce was very young when Amy was born and Amy was brought up by her grandmother, Helen's mother. Amy was living with her mother when she began stealing from neighbours. She was eleven years of age at that time and was still stealing two years later when her mother was interviewed.

> I just didn't know what to do about it. I wanted the Family Services, you know, just take her off me because I felt like I was an unfit mother to look after her at that time which I was; I was smoking marijuana at that time myself. I was blinded. I didn't know what she was up to, you see, stealing and everything. But you see, I'm a new-born Christian now and God, He sort of opened my eyes up to see where I made my mistake. I was blinded by the drugs that I was smoking.

As Amy kept on offending, her mother became ambivalent about keeping her. She didn't want to give her up again, as she had to her mother when Amy was little, but she did not feel she was able to cope.

> The same hurt and bitterness just kept on coming back to me but at that time, see, I just didn't want to abandon her, put her on to someone else, you know. I wanted to look after her myself and at that time I didn't know what to do and I had no support . . . many a times I

wanted to commit suicide. I thought that was the only way out. But I don't know what held me there for Amy. Yeah, I thought of committing suicide many a time. I thought it would be an easy way of backing away from my problems, you know, away from the problem and if the Family Services take her and put her in a home, let the Family Services deal with her (Helen Joyce).

For Eva Marcos, the mother of Richard (17) and Tess (16), there was further humiliation in comparing her family's previous position with that it now found itself in their adopted country.

I was very ashamed, degraded, you know, because in the first place in the Philippines I have my brother who is a policeman and also we had a good family background at home . . . you know it is very shameful, it's a disgrace to the family. So even now, they don't know that my son has been involved with that kind of thing, otherwise they will say what kind of family you are. You are a bad parent, you know, because it's a disgrace over the family . . . we are very disappointed with the thing that happened for us. Especially, because Richard has a sister who has followed in his footsteps. The only difference is my daughter wasn't involved as seriously in break and enters, right, but she was involved in a drug addiction . . . ..We had a good family, we had a good relationship before and now she's breaking it because she said that at home here she is bored doing housework. Australians don't do any housework at home and for us, you know, that is our culture, that is our tradition. We had to discipline our kids to being hygienic to our house, you know. She reckons that Australians doesn't care about their home if it is messy, or whatever. She wants to do her own thing, going to her friends, taking some alcohol and drugs and things like that . . . .. My husband is irritable all the time. Yes. Very irritable and we always have an argument because maybe he is thinking what is happening (Eva Marcos).

Other parents try and keep the communication open by reasoning with their child. Ray and Donna Towner have a son, Brendan, aged 15, who was charged with 23 offenses of damage, break and enter, and stealing. As Donna Towner said,

There's no words to describe having to sit in the back of a police car with your child and be taken to the places where he has smashed cars, broken into buildings, stolen things and wreaked havoc, smashed plate glass windows. And, then, having to front the people that owned these buildings and be treated like you're the biggest piece of scum in the world. Ray (husband) didn't have to do that, he wasn't here, not when I had to go there. There's nothing that can describe how I felt when I had to go with Brendan and see what he had done. It was horrendous, it really was horrendous, and I suppose I would've liked to have belted the living daylights out of him, I truly would have (Donna Towner).

Yet, as her husband Ray said, they tried to reason with Brendan.

> We didn't go off our brain or anything like that at him and shout and yell at him. We took it quite well, you might say, calmly. We just asked him, 'why did you do it, what possessed you to do it?' and things like that. You know, we didn't kick him out because he'd done it, or anything like that. We went to court when he went to court to be by his side and give him moral support and all that type of stuff. There was no sense in going off the brain or belting him or anything like that for doing it. He was (then) a 14-year-old kid; he's not a kid really, he's a young adult. You know, we more or less told him that he's got to take responsibility for what he's done; you do the crime, you do the time, so to speak. But we had our own feelings, you know. I don't know what Donna felt, but I was kind of disappointed and down in the dumps about it. It's pretty hard to explain that, how you feel about it. You ask yourself 'what did I do wrong' and all this kind of stuff, you know. He's rebelling, that's about all, he wants to be one of the boys. The crowd he's getting around with was pretty well bad, you know, and he had to be one of the boys (Ray Towner).

Mary Smith also tried reasoning with her son, Peter (17), but without much success.

> Well, just talk to him that this wasn't acceptable, also about the dangers of drugs and that sort of thing, how it could affect his school work and just everything. He just wanted to go his own way. He said that we were old fashioned. He just wanted to go along with, you know, his so-called mates; it was just thrill seeking . . . he wasn't achieving at school or anything (Mary Smith).

Parents' reactions to offending

Parental reactions to the children's offending ranged from shock, upset, and embarrassment, to feelings of worry, despair, disbelief, fear, and concern for the young person's safety and well-being. After the initial feelings had dissipated, parents recalled anger as the dominant and residual emotion. While this anger was often directed at the young person involved in the offending, parents in the study thought long and hard about their own contribution to the events. '(I was) shocked, upset and hostile initially, but then as anybody does when you first find out something like that, you explode, and then after everybody had calmed down we sat around and discussed it' (George Carter, father of Mary, 14). One common reaction among parents was a feeling of aloneness, that their child's offending somehow isolated them from their families, their friends and their community. Brenda Jones said she felt 'like you're the only person who has ever gone through it, especially when you can't get help' and Ingrid Perkins felt 'I couldn't talk to anybody really. You know, I was thinking, oh, it was all my fault . . . so I didn't really turn to anybody.' For other mothers, like Donna Towner, the nature of her son Brendan's offenses meant that she couldn't talk about them.

> He was with kids who broke into the High School and did some damage over there. Well, our daughter was doing her senior year and there was no way she was telling anyone what her brother had done. And I was working in the school cafeteria. The woman that runs the cafeteria knew it was my son because I told her, she's a friend, and I was in that cafeteria when the teachers come down and they were talking about the damage that'd been done to the school. There's no way that I would've told them that he was my son because there's no way I could've handled their reaction. So, you know, we hid things (otherwise) it would just be so embarrassing (Donna Towner).

Other parents, rather than turning to professional counselors, looked to family and friends to help them understand what was happening.

> Well, there wasn't really anybody except the family and friends. My mother, she's had lots of experience bringing children up, having eight. She'd say, 'Look, don't blame yourself, you know, you're doing everything you can; you've brought him up the same way that you've brought the others up and you're not to blame.' She just used to just be there, you know, for me to talk to. The same with my husband's mother and friends as well. And my workmates. They used to get an ear bashing (Mary Smith, mother of Peter, 17).

Others did seek professional help, either through counseling or through support groups.

> I ended up having to have counseling once. Ray told me that I was going crazy. I probably was. I can't believe it can still upset me. It got to the stage where the counselor actually asked me if I was considering suicide. That sort of brought me around, because I said, 'There's no way in the world I'm going to take my own life; it's not going to stop him from doing what he's doing' and I started going to (a support group). That saved my sanity and that turned me around,

how I was treating him. If he wanted to do it then it was his responsibility to stand up and take the punishment and it wasn't my fault that he had to wear what he did. I was angry and frustrated and disappointed and it made me realize just how bad I felt (Donna Towner).

For one mother, it was only through her religious beliefs that she could cope with what had happened. Helen Joyce's daughter, Amy, aged 13, was notorious in her neighbourhood for her stealing. Her mother found solace in religion and left her daughter, Amy, aged 13, to her own devices.

Like I pray to God to help me, you know, to give me answers and it's right there in the Bible. Yeah. Like, He just lifted all the burden off my shoulders because I used to blame myself for when she used to steal. But now, when I gave my heart to Jesus, she knows if she gonna' go out and steal well, that's her own action and she knows the consequences what's going to happen to her, and I'm not going to be responsible for her anymore. It's her action, she's old enough to know what's right from wrong. Yeah. And my advice is to hang in there and the only answer to all my problem was God. Yeah. He solved all my problems and now I look back on all the mistakes I made and everything. He saved me (but) the Devil, he just want to control our thoughts and everything. That's what I think he was doing to Amy, controlling her mind, you know, controlling her mind, tellin' her to go and do this and that, (saying) 'your mother don't worry about you, she doesn't love you, she abandoned you before, so what gave her the right to come back into your life and try and control it'. Yeah. And I believe God just solved all of my problems. He was an answer (Helen Joyce).

A similar, but more secular response was given by Wendy Reynolds.

Running the household gets very hard. I mean, there are days where I just lock myself in the room and say, 'Bugger it, I'm not going to do a thing today,' and I don't worry about meals; I don't worry about the shop; I can't even cope with the dinner. I don't even think of it, you know. And I've got to say I've got a very good husband who will come home and say, 'I'll cook tonight,' which is more or less five nights out of seven. He's really good. He'll do a lot of washing. He helps me so much in that respect as far as household work goes and material things go, he's wonderful. Emotionally, though, we have a lot of problems. But, I think that I have a mechanism in my head that just sort of cuts things off. I think I've learnt that as a coping mechanism now. I never got into debt or anything, but I got very lazy, very withdrawn. I didn't want friends, I wouldn't go out because I just knew that I would be so embarrassed by my children. Lester's got to be in on everything. He's the boss, and he used to be very much a bully and something would always happen. Some little thing would always start and I'd end up having an argument with other people (Wendy Reynolds, mother of Lester, 12).

The Mackeys have their own ways of coping with 12-year-old Matthew's offending. When trying to talk to him does not work and they feel angry towards him they let off steam in other ways.

> I just shut it all up and think, you know, but I've got a good relief. I go out on every second Friday and I get pissed (drunk). I release the tension which is good, everything just gets let out on the dance floor (Flora Mackey).
>
> Oh, I get pretty frustrated. I go and see me mate across the road to have a chat, calm down, come back and everything's right again. I just need to calm down again. It gets to you that much you've just got to get out. I normally go for a ride or go over next door or go and kick the football around (David Mackey)

A typical response from many parents was to reason with their child, pointing out to him or her that what they were doing was wrong and what the consequences might be.

> Well, it wasn't a shock because I knew he was doing offending, but I was talking to him, telling him not to. 'Don't do that or you're going to get into trouble,' I basically said. 'Right, yours is the responsibility. If you choose to go out and offend, you've got to suffer the consequences.' I put it all back on him trying to make him responsible for it (Daniel Santorini, father of Paul, aged 17).

Why do you think talking to him didn't work?

> Because they look at us parents, us oldies, and say to themselves, 'They're not going to tell me what to do. I'm in charge. I'm going to run my life.' And that was Paul's basic attitude. So I thought, well, you'll go so far and then someone will stop you, and it won't be me because you won't listen to me (Daniel Santorini).

But placing responsibility on their son for his actions did not mean, as it had for Helen Joyce, that the Santorinis abandoned their child.

> Well, basically what we could do is to be there to pick him up when he went wrong and be there to support him. We had to sort of show him that he'd done wrong. But that's in the past; now we get on with the future and we try to forget about it. Hopefully he'll learn from what he's done (Jean Santorini, stepmother of Paul).

However, some children don't just keep their thoughts to themselves or walk away without replying. Brenda Jones found that her son, Tim aged 17, turned violent.

> They get very defensive and they get very aggressive; my son did. So it's a case of smashing and banging, and abusing; he's raised his fists to me a few times. He's never actually hit me. I've tried to get him out of the house and he just flatly refused to go. He finally decided that we've had enough and he left about four weeks ago. And it's absolute heaven. I feel like a great big weight has been lifted off my shoulders. It's wonderful now. I feel I can be firm without having to put up with the tantrums. Like, he's rung up a couple of times reverse charges and I haven't accepted the calls. He left to prove he could be independent, so I'm not paying for his phone calls. Little things like that that I can say no to, and I know I'm not going to have a full-blown tantrum (Brenda Jones).

Mary Smith had a similarly violent response from her son, Peter, aged 17. Peter spoke about harming himself and also physically threatened his mother.

> He was just wasting his life. It was very difficult to get him involved in something that he was good at. We'd build his confidence up; he'd just put himself down and say he was a failure, and he even talked about taking his own life, you know, at one stage. He didn't want to be helped. Yes. It was terrible. I mean the way he was towards me especially. He was just so abusive and at times he would hold a knife to my throat and just threaten to kill us. My husband found it very hard to cope with. He just wanted to go out and get away, you know, he just couldn't deal with it because he and his son were very close when they were younger and he just couldn't handle it. And, I was left mostly to cope with it (Mary Smith).

For one or two parents, the violence comes from them and is directed at their children.

> I just felt like tearing her apart and just giving her a bashing with my fist and everything. I just felt real angry inside and everything. I just felt like grabbing hold of her and just flogging the shit out of her. But I knew that I had to stay with her, see, she's the only child I got. Although I had all this frustration and anger, I didn't want to put her on to someone else and leave the problem with someone else. I wanted to deal with it, see if I could manage to get through all this. It felt like, Family Services this is your job, why don't you deal with it. But I didn't want to be like my mum. It all gets back to my mother, see. Well, I didn't want to do the same thing what she did to me (Helen Joyce).

Flora Mackey had the same feelings of violent anger.

> I got to the stage where I got that frustrated and I felt I just wanted to hit him and I rang up (a respite center). I said, 'Look, I'm going to kill my son if you don't get him out of my house. I am going to hit him if he's not out of my house.' So they turned around and they had to contact Family Services. Fine, do it, get him out of my face. If he'd a been here, I would have killed him. And I know it. And it's scary because I just get really angry (Flora Mackey).

Some other mothers, such as Donna Towner and Josephine Heatley, have struck their children in order to discipline them.

> I haven't hit him too many times. Only really hit him once; that shocked him because I said to him, you know, I'll take just about anything from him but I won't have him swear at me. And he swore at me, come out with 'eff' or something and I smacked him in the mouth, just a flick. I could've just about sat him on his backside with that, he was so shocked that I had raised my hand to him and I said, 'Don't you ever, ever swear at me.' I said, 'I will just about take anything from you, you're my son, I love you, and I'll be with you all the way, but do not swear at me.' He has not sworn at me since. It was only a tap but it floored him, it really did (Donna Towner).

Josephine Heatley voiced a complaint of a number of parents, sentiments often repeated in the local newspapers, that do-gooders, and in her case White do-gooders, had curtailed the rights of parents to physically discipline their children.

> I punched him (Nicholas) in the police car there last time. They asked me not to hit him; they said, 'We've got to protect him, too, Mrs Heatley.' It made me wild. I mean, I'm coming off on the worse end of the stick trying to tell my kid 'You can't go, boy, you've got to stay home' and then he doesn't listen. What can I do because the White man's taken it right away from me. Because when my mum said jump, we jumped. But today the kids when they want to go they go. It's only when they get in trouble they look for mummy. We were belted a hell of a lot when we were small. Now, and that's why the kids piss in our pocket today because they say you touch me, I can have you up for assault? Well, where's my right? How am I going to get through to this black kid being taught the white man's way of discipline? I come from a different culture from the White man. I mean the White man's saying to me as a Black person, 'You bring your child up the way I've been brought up.' You know, it don't work that way. I come from a different culture and that's our way of disciplining our kids. I reckon them kids should go back, you know, to the old traditions (Josephine Heatley).

Mary McLure had much the same reaction and opinion about her son, Cain (17).

> Then the language started and the verbal abuse got worse and he'd just go out when he wanted to. I slapped him across the face once and he sort of put his hands up to me, but he never actually hit me but threatened to. I don't think he was game enough, but, I mean, if he had've, he would have flattened me because he was quite a large boy.
>
> (They should bring) it back in that you were allowed to discipline your child and give them a good smack over the ear or a foot up the bum when they need it. Give the teachers back the responsibility of giving them the cane at school if they needed it. Stop emphasizing how much rights the kids have and giving the rights back to the parents of being able to discipline the child and know that you're not going to be taken to court for abuse or bashing them.
>
> And I think the old style of discipline, I think it was a lot better. I guess you can go overboard with abusing your child and bashing them, but I think there's a lot less of that than there is of parents being allowed to discipline their child or their kids in old-fashioned values of what we were brought up with when we were kids. I mean, we never back-chatted our parents or abused them; if there was a disagreement it was generally talked out. And you had the back-up of your neighbours and the rest of society (Mary McLure).

Admittedly then, some parents, as part of their attempts to change the behaviour of their children and out of frustration, physically struck their children. No parent admitted to extreme forms of physical punishment, and the parents who did hit their children were a distinct minority of those interviewed. However, these reactions, and the worry caused to parents by the offending, were caused by concerns of what might happen now that their child was committing crimes.

> Well, I think the fact that what he was doing was illegal. That it would lead to harder drugs. As far as I know he was only smoking marijuana, but I just felt it was just one more step to go on to the other things that they can pick up. There were a lot of concerns about him getting into trouble and sort of ending up with a record. There's a lot of things go through your mind; how you're ever going to cope with it all yourself (Brenda Jones).

Aftershocks

Following the initial shock and reactions to the young person's offending, some parents participating in the study initially believed, or at least were hopeful, that the first offense was an aberration, a 'one off' incident. Initially, there was a view that the penalty imposed would act as a strong deterrent to repeat offending. However, when the young person was issued with a warning or placed on a supervision order, all parents interviewed reacted adversely to the perceived leniency of the system. This was particularly crucial for parents whose children had been involved in minor offending for a number of years and had previously been interviewed or warned by police about suspected criminal activity with no action being taken. Parents reacted by trying to exercise more control over the situation and in particular the young person's behaviour, often with little effect.

Parents tried curfews (Carter, Watts, Towner), physical restraint within the house (Mackey, Joyce), ordering their child from the house (McLure) and even informing the police about their own and other young people's offending (McLure, Towner) in attempts to curb the offending behaviour. Interviews with these parents contradict the often repeated assumption that the parents of juvenile offenders opt out of their parental responsibilities. These parents demonstrated a high level of involvement with the young person in an attempt to address their behaviour. Their inability to do so reinforced any perceptions they may have had that they were failing in the jobs as parents.

As discussed earlier, parents of juvenile offenders have attracted a great deal of attention in regard to the provision of adequate care and supervision of their children. Parents interviewed were aware of being in the invidious position of being both the source and the saviour of juvenile delinquency (Carrington 1993: 76). In the main, conflict between the young person and the parents centred around parental expectation of the young person and the adherence to established household rules. These rules included coming home at a specified time, attending to household chores, informing parents of their whereabouts, and regular attendance at school. The rules extended to prohibiting the young person from using drugs or drinking alcohol inside and outside of the home. While all parents involved in the research identified conflict with their children over some or all of these issues, following the offense they tried even more rigorously to regulate the young person's activities.

Chris and Susan Watts, as noted in Chapter Five, identified over a number of interviews the types of strategies they employed. These ranged from actively monitoring John's behaviour, trying to reason with him logically about the type of kids involved in offending, through to encouraging his participation in discussion about his behaviour. The strategies the Wattses employed had little effect. John's offending continued and corresponded with increasing periods of absence from the parental home. When they believed that they had exhausted all avenues, they were advised by a local youth organization to stop running after their son and to get on with their own lives. As Chris Watts recounts,

> We were virtually told to wait until he hits rock bottom and virtually handle it as though we would always be there for him, but we weren't going to be running around the streets wrecking our own lives for him either. We were virtually told to get on with our own lives.

This account of the Wattses' attempt to reason with their son took place some time after John had begun offending. Their sense of parental responsibility can be contrasted with the opinion of the youth organization which saw their role in more passive terms. While they were well aware that their continued attempts to change John's behaviour weren't working, they resented being told to sit back and wait for him to hit rock bottom. As we shall see in Chapter Eight, the Wattses have articulated a common complaint of parents of juvenile offenders, that services are directed at the offenders while parents are marginalized and even ignored.

Consequences for the family

The young person's offending had consequences for the parents in terms of their 'sense of failure' as a parent, on their own interpersonal relationships, and on the relationships with their other children. Parents told of the deleterious influence the young person's behaviour and offending was having on younger siblings.

> We've got problems with his sister now. She feels that we let Paul get away with those things, so she thinks she can do them. She says Paul ran the streets, Paul did this, and she's the type of kid that her brother

is her idol. So, my big brother did this, I'll do it. We try to tell her your brother did it and your brother has realized it was wrong, so you shouldn't be doing it. But she can't see it that way. [But] it didn't affect my kids too much, though, did it? (Jean Santorini).

For Chris and Susan Watts, the stress of their son's repeat offending impacted on their marital relationship. John's offending amplified the differences between their parenting styles. Chris perceived Susan as 'soft on John' but admitted that he was 'much harder and black and white' about issues. This, and the lengthy period of active involvement in trying to control John's behaviour, led to a deterioration in their relationship and prompted them to seek relationship counseling (which they had to pay for and which they couldn't really afford). However, Chris was able to identify that, even at this stage, their focus was still on John. 'I mean, we have just spent two years from hell. Susan and I actually went for marriage counseling and we'd go there and sit down and spend the whole hour and a half talking about John.' However, Chris acknowledged that the counseling was beneficial to their relationship, even though it did not give them any pointers in dealing with John's behaviour. 'Oh, yes, it did help because there was a third person there who could say to me 'Okay, you can see how Susan felt about that,' or vice versa.' The Wattses also worry about the effects on their younger son, Paul. They acknowledge that John loves his little brother, but are worried about Paul's behavioural problems. Chris says, 'We do know that Paul did have a few behavioural problems because of the shenanigans that John has been up to.'

Other families had similar worries about the effect of one child's offending on other children's behaviour and attitude. Eva Marcos has already mentioned the negative effect of her son Richard's behaviour on his sister, Tess. Jean and Daniel Santorini had identical problems with their daughter: 'we've got problems with his sister now. She's the type of kid that her brother is her idol. So, my big brother did this, I'll do it' (Jean Santorini).
Donna and Ray Towner also had worries about their 15-year-old son Brendan's influence on his eight-year-old brother, Neil.

It's really, really hard. I mean, it's hard because we've got Neil coming up and he wants to do things that Brendan's doing and I'm finding

> that I'm now being very hard on him, I'm being very hard on him and so is Ray. He's paying a price for Brendan (Donna Towner).
>
> Young brothers, you know, look up to their bigger brother as a role model. Yet, Brendan don't care, he'll still swear in front of Neil and all that (Ray Towner).
>
> Yeah, he tells him about having sex (Donna Towner).
>
> And then he tells him all his episodes outside this house, you know, about his girlfriends and all that. Before you came here tonight the two boys out there were sitting on the front verandah blowing up bloody condoms into balloons (Ray Towner).

Jody Fraser, too, discussed the negative impact that James's behaviour had on her younger children: '. . . the other three look up to him and the way he acts and the way he talks and everything, they react to that.' Kathy Fleming had a more serious problem. Her daughter, Natalie (17), physically abused her younger sisters.

> It was just that conflict, continual confrontation. You couldn't leave her in the house alone with her little sisters. If I had to go to the shop, I had to take the little kids with me and leave her at home. I knew if I left her at home with the little ones I'd come home and one of them would have fallen over and been bruised and been pushed. I'd come home to a screaming house. So it was easier for me to take them away from the situation.

What sort of impact did that kind of difficult relationship with your daughter have on the family as a whole?

> Well, Bradley (her partner) was pretty good. I can't really say we had an argument. Bradley never saw the really bad behaviour that I saw; it was only towards the end, just before she actually left home, that he saw that side of her and I don't think up until that point he realized what I was going through every time he walked out of the house (Kathy Fleming).

Young people's offending behaviour was often resented by neighbours. The Mackeys had to move house because of Matthew's offending.

> I asked for a transfer. The neighbours were wanting to kill him. We had moved there before most of the people and I've been there nearly eight years. It was gradually getting worse and it was getting to the stage where he'd go to the next door neighbour's place and break in. All of them used to talk to me, but if Daniel so much as walked in that

yard or past the yard it was, 'Get off my property.' Yeah, so it was Daniel (Flora Mackey).

Yet, not all aftershocks were negative. For Brenda Jones, her son Tim's departure from the household changed for the better both the atmosphere and the quality of her relationship with her younger son.

> Well, you're so busy reacting to the noise and the tantrums and the attention seeking that the other kids tend to miss out on a lot. They tend to get overlooked and you find yourself so stressed out coping with his constant noise and pressure that you just don't want to handle anything else anyway. Now Tim's out of the house everybody is relaxed. I'm building up a good relationship with Brian (brother) now. I found that Brian got dragged into it, too. You sort of look at him and think, 'Are you doing the same thing?' Whereas, really I knew he wasn't. But you find yourself doubting the other kids as well. As I said before, I didn't really know Brian. I'm getting to know him now. I don't think there's been one raised voice in the house since Tim has gone. Everything is peaceful and calm, stress free.

Interestingly, mothers seemed better able to verbalize the effects of their children's offending. Mothers were often very vocal in describing and analyzing family life subsequent to their children's behaviour. It would be a caricature to contrast mothers' articulateness with fathers' inability to speak about the situation of offending children, often sons, as a number of fathers in this study were quite able to describe and analyze what had happened. However, some fathers seemed to withdraw into themselves after their children became involved in offending. Thus, Eva Marcos, spoke of her husband becoming 'irritable.' Mary Smith's husband 'switched off' after their son, Peter (17), began offending.

> My husband? Oh, a lot of the time he'd just switch off. He'd get angry at him when it first started. Or he would drink, he turned to drink, too, you know. But it was very hard for him to deal with it, especially coming from being in the military and having his standards. It was very hard to deal with a son who was going right against his everything (Mary Smith).

Other couples felt the strain in their own relationships as they disagreed on what steps to take to control their child's offending. The following dialog occurred during an interview with the Towners.

> It didn't really affect our relationship (Ray Towner).
>
> We were fighting a lot (Donna Towner).
>
> Were we? (Ray Towner).
>
> Yes (Donna Towner).
>
> Not physically, just arguing though (Ray Towner).
>
> Verbally; verbally arguing (Donna Towner).
>
> Oh yes, like sometimes she'd be sticking up for him when I'm saying, you know, kick him out, and next week I might be sticking up for him and she'd be saying, 'No, I don't want him here, he's disrupting the household,' and all that kind of stuff (Ray Towner).

The Santorinis had much the same problem. What do families do when they can't agree on the best course of action, in their case about their son, Paul, 17? The Santorinis split on fairly stereotypical gender lines that meant that the brunt of the problem was borne by the mother.

> We got to the understanding that everybody is an individual and she's got her opinions and I've got mine . . . I'd say, 'Paul, you did it, that's your problem. You've got to handle it.' And Jean would pick him up and sort of keep us in separate roles (Daniel Santorini).
>
> I was there to pick up the pieces, to try and help him if I could. I had a natural mother's instinct that, if one of your kids are in trouble, well, you pick up the pieces. That did cause a bit of argument with Daniel quite a few times because he felt that I was babying him and I shouldn't be doing it. It was making matters worse (Jean Santorini).

Children's offending has a very destabilizing effect on families. Commentary on juvenile crime tends to emphasize the effect on neighborhoods, businesses, people's feelings of personal safety and even a rending of the fabric of society. The parents interviewed for this project show an even greater effect on families' functioning. The next section briefly considers how parents sought help to cope with the trauma of their child's offending.

Seeking help

Parents acknowledged their sense of isolation in dealing with their child's behaviour and offending. They also told of the lack of support services and the stigma arising from being involved with the Juvenile Justice system. There was a pervasive sense of parents not wanting to involve family or friends, particularly when the offending continued. Brenda Jones particularly identified the lack of understanding from her family and their reactive responses.

> I talk to my sister, but she hasn't had to go through it. She was very sympathetic and supportive, but she didn't really have the understanding. My mother I didn't talk to because I just feel she couldn't cope with it because she's not young. My daughter I had a sort of talk to about it, but she's very unsympathetic towards her brother. She feels he should be locked up and that's it . . . It's something that I just felt I couldn't discuss with a lot of people. I think I've always coped with things on my own. I've always tried to handle things on my own. And I think it was just a carry over from that.

Jody Fraser, too, couldn't discuss James's behaviour with her mother. She placed her son's offending in relation to other events occurring in her life.

> Well, I can't talk to mum. Mum was very ill at the time and for a month and a half or two months beforehand, she'd been sick and she'd been in hospital. So I had her being sick to deal with; I had James to deal with; I had hassles with my own personal relationship to deal with because it seemed like every time I had a crisis with the kids for some reason, he felt threatened, or he felt that the relationship was threatened.

Two Aboriginal parents told of the support they received from their churches.

> I'm going on a different road and I'm going to church, you know, which is helping me a lot. I just reach out. I believe in Jesus, that's all, and he helps me in my life and I can pass it on to Robert, pass what knowledge I learn.

> I couldn't believe it when Robert walked out there to give himself to the Lord, too. I don't want to force him into anything, you know, it's up to him. Sometimes he don't want to go, you know, but then that's because he's still rebellious. And I hope he just learns something from all this, anyway (Ingrid Perkins).

Helen Joyce has come to religion after years of drinking and drug use and wants the same benefit she finds in religion for her daughter. However, it is the practical counseling from her pastor that she values.

> I just didn't know where to turn at that time or where I was going to go or where we was heading, for destruction, I reckon. And the church has given us a lot of support, like counseling. They wants to counsel

> Amy. The pastor wants to talk to try and help her. Well, she hasn't been talking about her problems and that's what we wanted him to try and organize because I feel like mad that she needs counseling before she end up doing something to herself (Helen Joyce).

There is a further feeling of isolation that has arisen from the lack of support services available to parents. Parents described many avenues to assist them with the young person's offending, but not many venues to assist them with their own grief. Support services identified by participants included the Department of Family Services, community based organizations with family mediation programs, dominant figures in youth organizations and a support group, Support for Neglected and Abused Parents (SNAP). Parents were critical of government bodies and community based organizations due to the narrow focus of the services offered. These services were viewed as only supportive of the young person but isolating of the family, or of providing programs which were contingent upon the willingness of the young person to participate.

All parents strongly identified the lack of support services for parents. The majority of participants dealt with the problem themselves, with varying degrees of anguish and success.

> I don't know whether you want to call that pride. I just felt that they were my problems and I could deal with them. And I've had nights where I've just cried and that gets rid of it until the next day. And then it builds up again. And then when you need to deal with it, you deal with it again. You know, I can be very cold and very cut off from people if I want to be (Jody Fraser).

While Jody was aware of a parents' support group (SNAP), she opted to rely on her own resources.

> I was actually given a card for the Abused Parents, but I never rang them. I don't doubt that those groups aren't good. I seriously thought about it because I just tried everything with him. Everything possible, didn't I? I did. I tried everything.

Brenda Jones expressed her concerns about the lack of support.

> There were a lot of concerns about him getting into trouble and sort of ending up with a record. There's a lot of things going through your mind. How you're ever going to cope with it all yourself. You feel like you're the only person who has ever gone through it especially when

you can't get help. So it was mainly the group (SNAP) I go to that I got the most support from.

A number of participants in this project were involved with a self-help group called SNAP (Support for Neglected and Abused Parents). The acronym conveys the message that the parents of offenders are as much victims as those whom the young people offend against. The group is self-regulating and relies for its philosophy on a concept derived from the United States called 'Toughlove.' As noted by Toughlove International,

> The Toughlove program was started in the 1970s by Phyllis and David York. The Yorks were family therapists who worked in one of the most famous drug and alcohol rehabs of its time, training counselors, working with clients and their families, and conducting a private practice, in addition to being State Drug and Alcohol Trainers for Pennsylvania.
>
> The ten Toughlove beliefs form the basis of the Toughlove program.
>
> 1. Family problems have their roots and supports in the culture.
> 2. Parents are people too.
> 3. Parents' material and emotional resources are limited.
> 4. Parents and kids are not equal.
> 5. Blaming keeps people helpless.
> 6. Kids' behaviour affects parents. Parents' behaviour affects kids.
> 7. Taking a stand precipitates a crisis.
> 8. From a controlled crisis comes the possibility of positive change.
> 9. Families need to give and get support in their own community in order to change.
> 10. The essence of family life is cooperation, not togetherness.
>
> Toughlove groups are all over the United States and Canada and many foreign countries including Australia, Germany, Korea, and Brazil (Toughlove International, 1998).

Kathy Fleming, mother of Natalie (17), was the Townsville Coordinator of SNAP. The idea came to Townsville from New Zealand and the SNAP group had been running in Townsville for four years. She spoke of her own frustration with her daughter and the need for a group that was focused on parents and supported them.

> Well, I know in my own experience I had been to school counselors, I've been to Family Services at one stage; psychiatrist; psychologist; child guidance; and it was all for the child. There is just nothing there to help the parent cope with what was going on. It would have helped I think if I'd been able to go to somewhere like Child Guidance and had them say to me, 'Well, you're not alone. There are other parents out there that are going through this.' But that was never mentioned. It was always, 'Oh, you're the only parent that we know that's got this problem.'
>
> When I first heard that this group was starting up, my father said he could see a change in me immediately, because before that I felt so isolated that I was the only person. But once the group started I realized I'm not alone.
>
> It is about parents getting together. The thing is that most of them had been along similar types of lines to me and really not getting that support that they needed. When they get to that group, they haven't got some professional going at them, that this is what they should be doing. People that are prepared to sit down to listen to what they've got to say, and say to them, 'Look, these are some of the things that we've tried that have worked. You could try something like that.'
>
> It's called Toughlove because it's very tough on the parents because they love their kids so much that they're going to be tough on those kids because they do love them. And it's actually not hard on the kids. It's harder on the parents. It's very tough on the parents.

In a letter Kathy Fleming wrote to a Townsville radio station after hearing criticism of the parents of juvenile offenders, the philosophy of SNAP, and the hardline position taken by SNAP parents are clear.

> SNAP is a group of caring parents helping each other come to terms with their teenagers' behaviour, and attempting to make their teenagers responsible for their own behaviour. SNAP is a support group for caring parents by caring parents.
>
> The majority of parents do care about their children and what they get up to, it is a minority that let their teenagers go and do as they please.
>
> My daughter was told she had the right to do what she wanted, but she was never told or taught that with the right came responsibilities, and now a long time down the track, the acceptance of responsibility is something my child still cannot do; if anything goes wrong, her immediate reaction is to blame someone else, no matter what has happened. The teenagers we are coping with refuse

to live by any rules. As teenagers, society seems to accept this as the normal thing for them to do as they spread their wings, but as young adults, society then expects them to buckle down and do the right thing.

As caring parents, we resent people who have no conception as to what some of these children can be like, telling us that we must be responsible for what our children do. It is just one more burden to contend with after coping with the behaviour and the abuse these children can dish out. How would you personally handle a situation where a child has been banned from going out, stood and abused you, and went out anyway to come home days later? If you laid a hand on that child, he or she can go to the police and have you charged with assault, or can go to one of the Children Services Departments to be patted on the head and told what dreadful parents they have.

Until you understand the whole situation and/or live with the kids we have, we don't feel you have the right to condemn us out of hand. We need help with and for our kids, not condemnation. Until this happens, our kids are not going to become responsible adults capable of accepting responsibility for their own actions.

We hope you can come to understand our point of view and realize there are two sides to every story.

Parents such as Ray Towner act/react from the Toughlove set of beliefs. He was more intent on teaching young people a lesson than supporting them, no matter what.

> The only way to do it is really hit them hard. Not community service because that's false because 90% of them don't do it anyway. No, shove everyone that goes through the courts who have ten crimes, put them in Cleveland for a month because they're locked up away from the normal society and the others will stop it. They don't want to go there. It's only because they've been getting away with it (Ray Towner).

Towner's stance can be contrasted with other parents, especially two Indigenous women.

What advice would you give to other parents who had similar experiences to you?

> Well, always to be there. You know, you know your kid's done wrong, but don't walk away and say, 'Oh, well, I can't accept what this fellow's done. I don't want nothing more to do with him.' No, that's not my attitude. I know in my heart my son done wrong and my son's got to learn the hard way, but he also needs his parents, well, his mum. And, you know, his aunties and uncles and grandma to visit for support. Don't walk away from them (Josephine Heatley).

Ingrid Perkins, another Aboriginal mother, had similar advice.

> We just got to talk to them. We just got to give them our love and show them that we care and then I think, you know, what else more can we do? We're just trying to show them the right track but we all got our own choices. They know what's right from wrong, too (Ingrid Perkins).

The differences between the two approaches are striking.

Conclusion

Having a child who is continually offending is a traumatic and unnerving experience. As one mother put it,

> I was really bad for two or three years there, I was really bad. Yep, I've just started getting some self-esteem back, I think, some self-image with the bowling and doing a bit of work and feeling a little bit more useful in life now. And I don't take the shit I used to take when I was younger. But when I was younger, like my first marriage, I was just a doormat and then the second marriage, you sort of wanted to grow but you couldn't. Now, I don't take shit off nobody, practically. So I think I've learnt a lot.
>
> I take a long time to think sometimes. It doesn't power out like it should. I feel sorry for my kids because they haven't had a stable upbringing. There's a lot of regret there for them. And it's too late to turn it back, so I feel really awful that I can't turn their childhood back for them (Wendy Reynolds).

The parents in this study contradict popular assumptions that they are uncaring and irresponsible. Their often poignant stories conveyed the effect of their children's offending on them and their families. While none of the families could be described as perfect, neither were they dens of iniquity and lawlessness. Overwhelmingly, these families gave the impression that they were absolutely law-abiding and were horrified that their children had become lawbreakers.

CHAPTER SEVEN

Finding Fault: Families' Explanations for Offending Behaviour

A significant factor in juvenile offending is blame. Parents blame themselves and their children; neighbours, newspaper editors, and politicians blame parents; social commentators blame the breakdown of the family and society. This chapter will consider parents and juvenile offenders' explanations of the causes of offending behaviour. In the light of political and media emphasis on parents' culpability, parents will reply to those who target them as the causes of juvenile crime.

Our underlying aim in conducting this research was to question some of the simplistic assertions about families and crime currently circulating in public discourse. Contrary to the view that crime can be attributed to parental neglect (as claimed in recent legislation) the parents in this study demonstrated a deep concern over the behaviours of their children as well as a willingness to meet conditions set by the court. At the very least parents did not appear indifferent to the actions of their children. This attitude suggests something different to the family-blaming assumptions in contemporary crime control discourse.

Parents' theories

As outlined earlier in the review of the literature on families, a multitude of theories have attempted to explain the cause of juvenile offending. These range from the 'broken family' (Utting, 1994, 1995; Young, 1996), sibling numbers (Laflore 1988; Tygart 1991; Farrington 1994), parental failure (Glueck and Glueck 1950; Laub and Sampson 1988; Junger-Tass 1994), to multivariate factors

(West 1982; Farrington 1994; Utting 1994, 1995). Families involved in this study also have reflected divergent views when explaining their children's offending. Their explanations fell into three main categories: intrapersonality psychological causes, explanations derived from family functioning, and external pressures that have had an effect on children's behaviour. It should be noted that not all parents articulated a theory about juvenile offending.

Six parents put forward psychological theories for their children's offending. Five of these offenders were male. The first mother, Maggie Webb, saw similar symptoms in her son, Carl (17), to those she has seen in her father and brothers.

> I can see personality traits in him that I can see from my father and my brothers. I've got four brothers and three of them, I would say, have problems with depression. My father has suffered with severe depression for 15 years. My mother said the first 15 years of their married life was sheer hell and dad was under doctors for years and years and years, until in his later life when he sorted himself out. I had a good family doctor at the time and I would talk to her and I'd say, 'I look at him (Carl) and I can see my family, my father. I can see my brothers.' And she'd try and explain to me that some of it is genetic, some of it is environmental.
>
> Carl should have been under medication. My doctor diagnosed him as being depressed. He was suicidal at the time. He needed to go on medication but at that time he was also into drinking and you can't take medication and drink. So, he made a decision. It was the drugs or the alcohol and the alcohol won at that time. He was not interested in getting himself well, because depressed people don't think that they're sick.

Yet, despite her rational explanation of her son's behaviour, Mrs Webb cannot ignore her own insecurity that perhaps it was her fault, as a mother.

> (Speaking of herself), You just take it as it comes and you try and deal with it as best you can at the time. I'm not saying that I'm the best of parents. I've probably got a long way to go, but I did the best I could. There's probably things that I could have done differently. I hope that in years to come that he'll look back on that time and realize that there was a lot of support for him through that time (Maggie Webb).

Brenda Jones, too, described her son's behaviour within the context of a long-term psychological disorder. In her case, however, her assertion of the psychological cause of his offending was not supported by a counselor he visited.

> So with him (Tim, 17), it wasn't actually the offending, it was his behaviour from when he was little that caused the problems. Offending just made it worse. It's just something he's always done since he was little. Ever since he was about 12 months old I've been to doctors, the odd psychologist trying to get help. And I've never had it. I talked him into going to a counselor about August last year and she was only a young person and she didn't have any kids. I feel he's Attention Deficit Disorder and I've always said there's something wrong, and she spoke to him for an hour and rang me up and said she tested him and there was no way he was ADD, that there's nothing wrong with him. So I begged to differ and told her she didn't know what she was talking about; she didn't have to live with it. And she told me I didn't know what I was talking about . . . You can't GET any help; I've never had any help for him. About three years ago, I got a referral to a doctor in Townsville that deals with a lot of the Attention Deficit kids, and he wouldn't see him because he was too old. So that was the last thing I tried apart from the counseling.

Kathy Flamingo's explanation for her daughter, Natalie's (17), offending was a brain dysfunction, or a disjunction between what she knew to be right and what she did.

> She knew what she had to do, so I think there was a dysfunction between the brain and the hands. The brain knew what she had to do but the hands couldn't do it and she just decided that she had rights and she was going to have those rights. She wasn't going to have any of the responsibility that went with those rights and it made continual confrontation.

Wendy Reynolds's son, Lester (12), unlike Tim Jones and Natalie Fleming, had been given a medical diagnosis of ADHD, Attention Deficit Hyper Disorder. However, his mother was skeptical of the diagnosis, seeing the label as merely a new name for an old symptom.

> He had a car accident when he was two years and nine months, and he was on life support for 24 hours. He had severe brain bruising and he didn't come back to consciousness and start talking for about three days; so I personally think that it comes from that. They've given it the label ADHD, Attention Deficit Hyper Disorder (smiling as she speaks). Yeah, I mean, I don't disbelieve in it, and I don't believe it. It's very hard for me to say what I think. There's always been children like Lester since way back; it's just now they've all given them a label, I

think. It used to be hyperactive kids. Now it is ADHD (Wendy Reynolds).

Cain McLure (17) was a moody young man who verbally abused his mother, often in front of his friends. He had been diagnosed as hyperactive when very young.

> I'd been to the hospital when he was very young to the psychologists, psychiatrists. I was told that because of his behaviour, he was diagnosed as hyperactive. He was on the go all the time, he just wouldn't stop. He'd throw tantrums if he couldn't get his own way. But they would tell me that it was my fault and Cain was blaming me because his father was away (his father worked away for six weeks and then had six weeks at home). So he'd put on these temper tantrums. I don't know how many times I've walked away and left him in the supermarket and on those stupid bloody rides that they put out the front. He'd get on one and you'd give him a ride, but he wouldn't get off . . .
>
> If he couldn't get his own way, he'd hit his head up against a wall, he'd throw himself down. He was quite abusive towards himself; he'd bruise himself and it would look like I'd bashed him. He'd lay down on the floor and he'd just constantly bash his head on the floor. He'd kick the doors. He has broken glass. He's put his foot through a wardrobe. He'd get in the car and he'd lock himself in the car on really hot days and he'd stay in there screaming. All he had to do was open the door, and he knew how to do it, too. I don't know if it was attention thing (ADD), or whatever, but finally he was diagnosed as being hyperactive, and he was put on a special diet. It was a matter of finding out what foods really affected him and take them out of his diet. His behaviour did come a lot easier to handle and it was a lot better. This was sort of up until the other two were born, but then by that time I was aware of what he couldn't have and could have with his diet (Mary McLure).

However, there was a more poignant reason for Cain's misbehaviour. His father and his paternal grandparents blatantly favoured his younger siblings over him. Possibly, this was because of his misbehaviour but this favouritism only added to his isolation.

> My husband at the time preferred to play around with the younger ones, when he came home, and he really couldn't be bothered with Cain. And, after the little ones were born, his grandparents also showed more favouritism toward them than Cain. If there were any gifts or anything for birthdays or Christmas, they'd go and buy expensive presents for the little ones and cheap ones for Cain, but

always leave the price tag on all of the presents so I could see and Cain could see how much they spent on the younger ones and how little they spent on him. And I thought, he must have felt that he was being pushed aside because the younger ones had taken over in his father's eyes and in the grandparents' eyes. So, his offending could have been for attention.

Cain didn't know how to reach out; he wasn't a kid that would open up freely with his emotions, or how he was feeling at the time, or if he was anxious. He seemed to be in competition all the time for affection with the younger ones. With my ex-husband being an engineer, Cain wasn't very mechanically minded, so if he didn't show any inclination toward that area, my ex-husband didn't really want to know (Mary McLure).

A further psychological reason, the need to show mastery of a skill, was put forward as a reason for their son's offending by Jean and David Santorini. Their son Paul (17) did not excel at school but he did excel at breaking into houses. Initially when asked about why they thought Paul was offending, they replied that it was peer pressure. Then, with a certain pride, David Santorini related how Paul, who was not expert enough to be chosen for school sporting teams, chose something he was good at, housebreaking.

When he went out housebreaking he was a total success. And that was his reason; if I can't succeed (at school sports), I'll go to something I can succeed in, and he was a brilliant criminal. Even the police told him that. He was brilliant. When they recognized who was doing it, they solved three-quarters of the unsolved crimes in Townsville.

He ended up safe breaking at the age of 15; that's what he got into. He was an expert. They knew he was doing it, but they could not prove it. He was an expert at it; the whole reason for him doing it was because he could succeed at it. He went to play football; they left him on the sidelines and, after going to all the training, he didn't succeed at it. But the thing he could succeed at was breaking and entering and stealing. And he was brilliant at it (David Santorini).

The six parents who have given psychological reasons for their children's offending locate the cause of that offending within the personality of the offender. The flaw, apparently, is genetic or physical or compensatory. The next group of parents see the cause of their children's offending within the dynamics of family living.

Perhaps the family with the most problems in their family life were the Mackeys. Flora Mackey catalogues a list of critical incidents that, she thinks, not only influenced her son, Matthew

(12), but created a climate in which his offending was more likely to happen. The first factor was Matthew's rejection and then abandonment by his father.

> But I think I was more pissed off at his father for the way his father treated him. He just treated him like shit. He wouldn't take him anywhere. Wouldn't do nothing with him. If Matthew would ask to do something, he said, 'No, you're not doing nothing.'
>
> Jim (the father) was going to get a job and send for us, he was supposed to go down there to look for work. That was the only reason he went down there, and he was supposed to send for us. About three months afterwards, it's 'Oh, I'm getting married again.' And Matthew just lost the plot, started offending really badly, breaking into houses and schools. When Jim pissed off, that's when he (Matthew) started being a proper little shit (Flora Mackey).

The second factor was Matthew's hyperactivity.

> And the other excuse is, 'Oh, I'm hyperactive.' He knows he's ADD and he thinks he can get away with what he does. So that makes it worse. He can't concentrate when he has to sit there for any length of time; in one ear and out the other; he's got a tremor; he just goes absolutely troppo without his tablets. He's on Ritalin to slow him down, but I think it makes him figure things out easier, getting to the point where he can think about what he's doing. Now that's a scary prospect.

The third factor was violence by Matthew's father towards his wife and Matthew.

> (Matthew) thought the family would last forever, that didn't help, no. The thing is he knew what his father was capable of too, hitting him and me. That's why I more or less tried to keep the kids in their room when he did start, you know. Matthew would be the one that would come out and try and stand in front of him. So Matthew knew what his father was like, but he still loved him.

The fourth factor was the apparent failure of Family Services to have a psychiatric evaluation of Matthew carried out. Mrs Mackey suspects that there is more troubling Matthew than ADD. The fifth factor was the adrenaline rush she suspects Matthew gets from offending.

> The Department of Family Services were supposed to hook it up that Matthew had a psychiatric evaluation. Three times the Court has asked for Matthew to have a psychiatric evaluation and they still haven't done it. That's [also] what's pissed me off. If they'd have done

> that, maybe they'd have found out what the causes were other than ADD; there's got to be something up there that's kicking in on him. And they've left it that long that it's habitual now.
>
> [Offending] is like a big adrenaline rush for him that he can go and get a fix any time, you know. And I think that's all it is now, a bit of adrenaline; it's fun for him, it's just a habit. It's something that he can't break. It's like trying to give up smoking when you've been smoking for 20 years (Flora Mackey).

Finally, the sixth factor was the realization by Matthew himself that circumstances, including his own offending, are leading him on and that he appears powerless to do anything about it. 'Oh, but, he knows; he's even turned around and said he knows he's doing it but he just can't stop it' (Flora Mackey). As Mrs Mackey so rightly said, 'I'd say there was four or five factors, but buggered if I know what.'

While Matthew Mackey's circumstances may be a good example of multivariate factors that lead to juvenile offending, another family admitted that neglecting a child could lead to that child offending. This example comes very close to the blameworthy parents often depicted in the media. Ingrid Perkins admitted that her son, Robert (15), was neglected because of her drinking and drug taking.

> I been drinking a lot and I believe doing all those things might have triggered him off. I never took notice of him, or tried to help him when he was going to school. I just, sort of, didn't care much, really. I was on the grog, you know, alcohol. It might be because I was on to that, and turning away from him, it might have affected him. He may have wanted my attention and I didn't give it to him because I was more worrying about other things. Pressure, you know, pressure was here for me because I never knew the responsibilities of living in a house and taking care of a house; it was like a big thing for me, you know.
>
> Yeah, I was sort of drugging on, too, you know, mixing all that up, yeah. But I just couldn't get away from it, you know. He seen me doing wrong things, so he probably thought, 'Oh, well, if she can do the wrong thing, my mother, you know, why not I do it, too.' So I believe all these things were going on in his mind, too, you know (Ingrid Perkins).

Young people appear very susceptible to great changes in family functioning. Death, separation, and births reconfigure family patterns that may have appeared set forever. Angela Ralph, for example, felt that her daughter, Helen (14), was not only 'in the wrong crowd at that time and in the wrong place at the wrong time' but vulnerable to deaths in the family as a destabilizing factor in her behaviour.

> I think because I lost my mother, that was her grandmother, in 1993 and then having to lose a brother, which was her uncle; I think she might have felt angry because of what happened. Because the death of her grandmother and uncle, she was very close to them and she kept that inside her and never opened up to anyone about anything. Maybe, I think, that's the reason why she could have offended in that way (Angela Ralph).

Not only separations but new partnerships were destabilizing for some children. Paul Santorini (17) began offending after his father married Jean. The Santorinis felt his offending may be a bid for attention.

> Did we do something wrong that he was thinking, 'You know, I'll fix these two?' I don't know what was going through his mind. That's what was going through my mind. I thought he was getting even because we got together; he maybe felt more rejected because he's sort of been through that before. He might think I'm going to get rejected again. This is my way of getting attention. I'll get them two apart to sort of get the attention for me. I don't know. That's what was going through my mind (Jean Santorini).

New additions to the family can also change family dynamics. The Towners told how their son, Brendan (15), changed after his brother was born.

> You see, our youngest child is nine years, seven years younger than Brendan and Brendan really started playing up when Neil was born. So we've had trouble with Brendan since. Neil's nearly nine, so we've been having problems at school since then. Really, I have no idea. Maybe he was looking for attention. It could've been something as simple as looking for attention (Donna Towner).

Although, as with other families, sometimes a catalyst was added to a volatile mix.

> Steepen is my sister's boy, the sister that died. He's the eldest of her four children and he was living with my mother, and he didn't like the way he was being treated, and he was basically doing what he wanted, when he wanted, whenever he wanted, and he rocked up here one day and asked if he could stay and I said yes. When he came to live with us Brendan started running away. He ran away 11 times, I think, in about three months. He just continued to run away (Donna Towner).

For other families, it was not external factors that altered the family dynamics but internal inconsistencies. In Susan Wattses case, the lack of discipline within the home was viewed as the determining factor in her son's offending. 'I think we should not have been so easy. Like, we tried to give him everything that his little heart desired. We bought him everything and let him go everywhere.' The issue of discipline and perceived comparative freedom of today's young people was identified by John's grandmother, Maureen Williams, as a cause of juvenile offending. As a widow, she had single-handedly raised her own four children and identified this as her point of reference. While she acknowledged that her daughter had tried everything to change her grandson's behaviour, she was generally critical of the lack of supervision and the impact of working parents on today's young. In this opinion, she reiterates views widely propagated in the media.

> Well, they don't seem to worry what their kids are doing. They go to work; the kids are home; they don't worry what they are doing when they're home; they don't check on the kids; if they go out, they come home when they feel like it. The kids are left to do what they like, left up to their own devices, which is pretty sad for our teenagers.

Parents, while not completely agreeing with this viewpoint, are nevertheless susceptible to the apparent logic of the position. Brenda Jones reiterates a common feeling among the parents in this study, the feeling that, somehow, it has been their fault. At the same time, her head tells her that it is not her fault at all. Her stance is reminiscent of the Toughlove beliefs.

> For a long, long time I felt very guilty about the way he's like he is, and I've learned that I don't have to feel guilty. It's not my fault he's like he is. He was born that way and he's got to learn to control himself and accept responsibility for himself. And I can't do that. I've taught him right from wrong. He knows right from wrong. It's up to him. I can't be there 24 hours a day, and I can't be held responsible for a lot of the things he does.

Chris Watts was also aware that his stepson, John (17), did not treat his offending seriously. On the one hand, Chris expressed some ownership for John's behaviour; however, this was tinged with frustration due to his inability to influence John and the reflection of this impotence upon him as a parent.

> We don't think that we're blameless, that's for sure. We feel that there's got to be some blame rested upon ourselves. I really felt that the only answer was to show to him that he had a home where he knew where he stood, and he just couldn't get away with things. Whereas he feels that he could tell us anything and he'd just tell us what we wanted to hear, and go and do whatever he liked.

Yet, when asked specifically to reply to those who would say that juvenile offending is the parents' fault, Susan Watts denied such a simplistic link.

> Well, I think that there is cases when it is the parents' fault. But there is many, many varied cases where it might be a combination, where it might not have nothing to do with the parents. You cannot pinpoint anything specific because each person is an individual and each child is a small adolescent and there is so many different and varied things that tip them over: drugs, alcohol, family. You know, it could be anything. So they can't just say the family.

Her mother, Maureen Williams, supported her daughter to a certain extent. While she admitted offending can be the result of chance, earlier she had blamed the pressures of modern living and another time economic conditions, she also identified factors that blame parents such as spoiling children or not providing direction for children. Tentatively, she proposed,

> You see, you just don't know. It's like a lottery. You'll see a house full of kids and they're great. They don't do anything wrong. They get good marks at school. They work together. Then you'll see a house with one or two children but both of them will be off the rails. Why? We don't know. They have everything they want, and maybe that's it. They get too much too soon and they when they get to 13 and 14, they've got most of it. They've had most of it and they don't know what to do with their time, their time has been filled in for them. They can't think for themselves in their spare time. They need someone to tell them what to do. I don't know if that makes sense . . . It's not always the parents' fault. I thought that years ago, I thought it's the parents. But then when we got this trouble with John, Susan has done everything that she possibly can to try and keep him—I don't know if he feels that way—to keep him out of trouble, but it hasn't worked.

Yet, with some parents, there was always that worry that they hadn't done enough.

I'll admit that I haven't spent as much time with him as I should. I've probably left it a bit too late. But even now I ask him to go fishing and he'd rather be running around the streets with his mates or girlfriend or anything like that. I've left it too late, I think. I haven't spent enough time with him (Ray Towner).

And Jody Fraser also reflected upon her role as a parent. 'You can't help but blame yourself. I did a lot of soul searching . . . I tried to see where I'd gone wrong . . . I tried to work out what had led to this.' In addition to intrapersonal and intrafamily factors that parents felt had precipitated offending behaviour among their children, some other parents identified a range of external factors they felt had been instrumental in causing their children to offend.

Josephine Heatley, for example, identified Nicholas's peers, 'his mates,' as factors. 'He chose to mix with the wrong crowd and look where it got him. I mean, I said don't drink, but nobody listened to me. No one listened to me. When the kids are set in their ways they just go that way and when they get into trouble, then they look for mum then.' Helen Joyce also mentioned peer pressure on her daughter, Amy (13). Working mothers, secularism, permissiveness, television, unemployment, poverty, disadvantage, boredom, and disaffection have all been blamed for the apparent slide into lawlessness. Particular attention, however, has been focused on the family. Crime has been attributed by politicians, shock-jocks, and social commentators to family break-up/breakdown, lack of parental control, responsibility, and discipline. Governments in America, Australia, and Britain have introduced tough new laws to punish the archetype beloved of the media, the Fagin-like adult who has children do his stealing.

> A lot of other teenagers used to push her up, see, but it all came down to she was taking the rap for everybody else. I used to say that to the police, 'Why don't you go and question these other people who was with her,' but they thought that she was making it all up. And there was an adult staying at the same place, a fully-grown woman in her 30s. And she used to take Amy up to the Hospital mainly to see a lot of the people. Amy used to steal money off the sick people and she would just take the money off Amy and go to the Casino and gamble it all. She had some kind of control over Amy. Money for the Casino, would you believe that?

Peer pressure was also a factor in Luke Ryan's offending, according to his parents.

> As soon as he hit high school, I found that he started getting into stealing and doing breaking and entering. It had a lot to do with the friends that he was mixing in with, too. He said it was out of boredom. All the time there was always the same children that were getting into trouble. Getting called to court all the time. It was the same little gang that they had. Yeah. I suppose he got bored, then, you know. Peer pressure, it might be somebody older than him say, 'Oh, we dare you to do this.' It's just that he just drifted off on the wrong track there. Easily led. Yeah. If you've got categories there, I'd put him under that, 'Easily Led' (Norm Ryan).
>
> He realized when he was in the home he said, 'I know, mum,' he said, 'now, they're not really friends.' And both of us said to him, 'Well, you're the one who took all the rap for everybody else.' We said, 'Now you know who your friends are' (Edna Ryan).

Boredom, coupled with non-attendance at school or unemployment, was also a recipe for offending. Thus, Jody Fraser identified a range of systemic social problems she felt had contributed to her son's offending.

> I think he was at the stage where he was fed up with school. He was sick of living in a situation where there were rules and regulations. You see, even though they had rules and regulations at the youth shelter, they still had all day to do what they wanted when they wanted . . . They're bored. I mean, if they're on the dole they haven't got a great deal of money. That's asking for trouble. They see something, they're going to start shop-lifting. They're going to start stealing cars because they're bored. They don't offer the kids anything.

Certainly, lack of ready money, even poverty, could be a contributing factor to juvenile offending. Lyn Butcher told of how her son, Tom (16), began stealing so he could have money like the other richer children at his boarding school.

> I think he first offended because he needed little luxuries that the non-Indigenous kids had when they were sent to boarding school. But he was never one to ask for anything. I would try to send food parcels and money when possible. When he started offending in Townsville, I first thought it might be a one-off thing; he might get this out of his system, but it just got worse. I talked to a work mate who was going through a great ordeal with her brothers and the police. Just having her listen made me feel a lot better. My son would pretend he was going to school, but would wag (truant) just to be with his mates at

the mall. I have no idea why my son continues to offend. When I ask why, I never get a reasonable answer (Lyn Butcher).

Finally, in a traumatic example of external forces changing the behaviour of a young person, Mary Carter (14) began offending after she and her younger sister were sexually abused by a family friend. Her mother and stepfather told what happened.

> The offending started this year when she was sexually abused by an old friend of the family they used to call 'uncle.' And then when he basically walked out of the court room, she started offending (Vicki Carter).
>
> He got two years probation and part of his probation was that he was to have no contact with us. He was to cross the road if we were on the same street. Actually, we don't discuss that in the house and that's why I didn't mention it earlier on because I'd forgotten all about it (George Carter, stepfather).
>
> And when they used to go down to their father's and spend the weekend or holidays there, they had to basically go past his place to get to their father's place (Vicki Carter).

So that would have been difficult for her.

> Yeah. It wasn't just her, it was one of her other sisters as well, but she refuses to talk to anybody about it. If she had've spoken, he would have gone to jail because the medical evidence was there on her, but not on Mary. Danielle has been very disruptive and everything at school, fighting.

How old is Danielle?

> She's eleven. I'm going to start crying . . . But we still come down hard on them (for offending and disruptive behaviour), hey? They don't get let off lightly around here because of that. They still get their punishment and everything like that. They still get everything that the others get, so there's no difference (Vicki Carter).

Overall, parental explanations for juvenile offending behaviour mirror the complexity of the literature. Some children have been disruptive all their lives, others appear to have had some sort of catalytic experience that has tipped them over into offending. Some explanations emphasize the psychological, others the functioning or lack of functioning of the family, others external traumas or circumstances. The pain and the incomprehension of parents are apparent in these accounts, and no one account captures adequately their experiences. The next section will consider some explanations for their offending from the offenders themselves.

Offenders' theories

Very few of the young people explained to their parents why they were offending and, when they did, they tended to be dismissive of their parents' concerns. Brenda Jones described her son Tim as having particularly trying and violent behaviours throughout his childhood. This had been the source of much personal anguish. Prior to Tim's arrest for drug related offenses, Brenda had been aware of his involvement in minor crimes which he had got away with. She expressed her anger and frustration about being accused by her son of overreacting. 'I was upset, angry with him for putting me through it, helpless because he didn't particularly seem to want any help. He told me it was not my concern.' As part of the interviews for this project, occasionally the young people concerned sat in or took part in the interviews. This was not planned, as the focus was on the experience of the parents. However, young people's explanations for their offending offered a suitable counterpoint to that of their parents. Five young people spoke to the researchers (Mary Carter, James Fraser, Robert Perkins, Brendan Towner, and John Watts).

While Mary Carter's parents felt her offending had been caused by her sexual assault, she had a different explanation. First, she told the interviewer that her offending had begun many years before.

> Oh, the first thing that happened was when I was about year four or five when I was riding to school. I walked into a news agency and stole some crayons and stuff. And then from then on I've just been stealing everything, anything. Well, it was like every single day, all day, but now I don't do it.

When pressed to say why she stole, Mary asserted, 'It was just the kids that I was hanging around with. The way I see it is, kids just steal because they want to do it and because of the way they are.' Three times she emphasized that children steal 'because they want to do it and because of the way they are.' Mary did not think that young people offended because their parents neglected them. 'The way it could have helped me back then was just to find a new group of kids to hang around with. Ones that weren't bad and just stealing and stuff' (Mary Carter).

Jody Fraser recounted changes in her son James's (16) behaviour which led to him leaving home, living in youth accommodations and eventually 'on the street.' When James was arrested after a high-speed police chase, she was initially very concerned for his safety and relieved that there had been no casualties arising from the incident. She described her own anger and frustration at James's unwillingness to discuss his involvement in the incident and his lack of recognition that the offense was serious. 'This was where I think all the anger came from . . . at that stage he had a very bad attitude. You know, he didn't want to talk about it. Everything was just a bit of fun . . . it was a buzz. You know, that was how they brushed it off. It was just fun.'

James Fraser had a different recollection. Following his arrest, he was initially concerned about the impact the offense would have upon his mother and his siblings. He explained his unwillingness to discuss the incident with his mother in terms of taking responsibility for his actions.

> . . . about mum I thought, Oh, she is going to be so disappointed, but mainly I thought about my little brother and sister and if they found out what they'd think of me because, my little brother, he looks up to me a fair bit. I just wanted to have some fun, and I thought if I move out of home then I take control of my life. I decide what happens when I go out, that way I take some responsibility for myself. Whatever I do, then I take the responsibility for it.

When asked why he offended, James replied in terms that centred on the short-term excitement he got from the offending. He spoke about the high-speed car chase and its aftermath. His statement corroborated his mother's estimation that he did it for fun.

> The biggest adrenaline rush I ever had before that was probably jumping the biggest jump at the BMX track and, I mean, that's like a two second adrenaline rush; bang, that's it, it's over. And then when (friends) Jimmy and Bill were talking about doing this and that and all the stuff that they'd done, the way that they said it, it made it sound real cool.

> So, the night that we stole the car, and when we were actually in it, the adrenaline, my heart, it felt like it was coming out of my chest, that's how fast it was beating. All the mates that I used to know, they never used to have cars or anything, and so I never used to go driving, thrashing it, like the way that we did that night. Oh, just that night, it was the most fun night that I've ever had but also the worst night I've ever had. I mean it was fun while I was in the car because I thought, yes, this was cool, I'm never going to get caught; it's going to be great. And then it was the worst night because then the coppers (police) actually caught us.

Robert Perkins (15), whose mother felt she had neglected him, stole out of boredom and poverty. He mainly stole jewelry (shoplifting) and bicycles 'and just a lot of little things.' When asked why he did it, Robert replied, 'Oh, nothing to do and just can't afford them things that I stole.' Despite his mother's assertion that she neglected him, Robert's recollection was that 'She used to just say it was bad doing that and she used to go on about jail and everything.' When Robert was asked if that made any difference to him, he replied, 'Not really. I just didn't want to listen.'

Another 15-year-old, Brendan Towner, also committed offenses because he was bored; it was 'just something to do.' Some idea of the opportunistic nature of this offending was given in his account of a night's excursion.

> The same fellow that I got into trouble with the first time, he come over and said, 'Oh, come on, do you want to come over and see Tony,' one of our other friends because we were going to go to a party. We went over there, got him, and we found out that the party wasn't on. So then we were going to go and see my girlfriend and on the way over we saw the lights on at the other friend's house so we stopped in there. She said, 'Oh, I'll come with you.' It was about 11 o'clock (at night), too late to see my girlfriend, and we went over to the high school playing basketball.
>
> Then this girl thought it would be a good idea to go and break into these classrooms; so she broke in there, and we all went in there. She couldn't find nothing in there so she took the clocks off the walls. She smashed them and then we went up to the other end of the building and she broke into another room there, and she took a little portable stereo and then we took that back to her house.
>
> Then we went up to the elementary school and because we were sitting at the front of the canteen, I said, 'I'm hungry, I'm going home,' and they said, 'No, don't go home, stay here.' So I stayed with them and they were looking for a way into the canteen.

They broke into the canteen and were arrested by the police as they left the school grounds. Brendan said he felt bad about the damage, but he could not help himself; 'When we did (the damage) it was really late at night and I was tired.' While Brendan's parents thought his offending behaviour was a cry for attention, Brendan's explanation was that it was 'just something to do.'

Brendan's older sister, Jodie, felt that part of the problem with Brendan was that he and his father had difficulty communicating. Brendan did not want to listen and her father, Ray, 'was not prepared to sit down and talk about it more. More times than not it turned into an argument. I just thought (Brendan) needed some sense knocked into him. I would have gladly done it.' Again, there were no deep reasons given by the offenders, merely that offending was just something to do.

John Watts (16) had been offending since he was thirteen. He used drugs such as marijuana and amphetamines. He had moved out of his parents' house and lived with his grandmother, who described him as moody; he's not a morning person, she said. He can fly off the handle, but then he'll come back and apologize ten minutes later. The way John described learning to drive from the older children was a pointer to how he began offending:

> You learn over the years. At first, you hang around with other people and they sort of show you and then you show the younger people and people your age . . . and it passes down. It's like a cycle, you know (John Watts).

When asked about why he offended, John replied in terms that spoke of offending's attractiveness to adolescents. His language is reminiscent of James Fraser's. '. . . stealing cars and shit, and not growing up. When you take them it's an all right feeling, just driving and shit.' John indicated that his offending was not considered serious because he was a minor. He was well aware that being a juvenile allowed him some leeway with the law. 'People go in and out of Cleveland (Youth Detention Centre) and that all the time, you know. But when you turn about 17 and that you sort of stop . . . you just sort of, just have fun until you're about 17 and then, you know, fun's over.' John was clearly aware of the consequences of attaining adult status. His grandmother, Anne

Boyd, thought his offending was caused by estranged relationships with his mother, Susan, over her marriage to Chris when John was eight years old. 'I think a little bit of jealousy is on John's side because he had his mum for so long, then Chris came along, and then Paul (his brother) came along. So instead of just having mum, he's had two others to share with mum. Maybe it's the wrong idea, but that's, I think, some of the basis for the problems.' John nostalgically wanted to return to the extended household of his babyhood, eight years before, when he was the only child and his mother, grandmother, uncles, aunts, and their friends seemed to party all the time. 'But when mum moved out of here, nothing ever happens over there. Now everything you do by yourself. You get lonely. Your brain gets lonely because you're always thinking inside your own head. But back then, when we had parties, we used to have heaps of people coming around' (John Watts). Susan Watts, John's mother, had believed that lack of discipline within the home was a contributing factor in her son's offending. Certainly, much of John Watt's explanation of his offending related to his wish not to grow up too quickly.

Only two main reasons were put forward by the five offenders to explain their offending. The younger offenders, Mary Carter, Robert Perkins, and Brendan Towner, were bored and it was something to do. Their offences tended to involve stealing. The older offenders, James Fraser and John Watts, sought excitement in stealing cars. It was the excitement, not what they stole, that gave them their satisfaction. Of the young people, only Robert Perkins (poverty) and John Watts (loneliness) were able to explain their offending in terms other than self-centred behaviour.

Blaming parents

The part allegedly played by parents in juvenile crime usually stops short of saying that parents are complicit in the crimes of their children. However, reports do focus on the apparent failure of parents to curb the antisocial activities of their children. During this research, local newspapers and state politicians targeted both parents and children for responsibility for juvenile crime.

> Parents in Townsville and Thuringowa may find themselves in the dock alongside juvenile offenders under new laws announced last

week. And they may also have to pay up to $5000 compensation where courts decide it is appropriate for crimes committed by a child. (State) Attorney General, Denver Beanland, on Wednesday launched the start of a four-week consultation period for amendments to the *Juvenile Justice Act* 1992. These changes are tough, yet fair, Mr Beanland said. (*Townsville Sun*, June 5, 1996).

Mr Beanland further commented that this important legislation will bring responsibility home to both the offenders and their parents. The community has had enough (*Townsville Bulletin*, May 30, 1996).

Parent blaming took on frightening proportions for Helen Joyce, who was accosted once by a neighbour and once more by two strangers about her daughter's stealing.

> I was at a shop and one fellow came down, and he accused Amy of stealing and I knew she did steal from him. He said, 'If I ever see her along the road again, I'm going to smash her hand with a hammer and break her leg and her kneecaps.' I was scared then. [Another time, two men from a vigilante group protecting houses from juvenile offenders] said why don't you control your daughter. Why don't you give your daughter discipline or keep her in your yard? If you don't keep her in your house, we're gonna bash her and abuse her. They were swearing and all. And at that time I just fell to pieces, you know. I just felt like I was going to have a nervous breakdown at that time (Helen Joyce).

Admittedly, this is an extreme case, at least in Townsville, but these punitive attitudes are produced and reinforced by the scapegoating speeches of politicians. This attitude was widespread in the community. Parent blaming was evident among the parents in this project. Brenda Jones, for example, believed there were parents that did not care about their children, although her real concern was parents like herself who do care but feel helpless.

> Well, I think that there are a lot of parents that don't bother about what their kids are doing. But the parents ... that do care, are helpless. There is not a lot you can do when your kid stands there and abuses you. And if you tell them they're not allowed to go out, they say, Well, I'm going anyway. And they go. How can you stop them?

The parents interviewed were vehemently caustic about the suggestion that parents were to blame for their children's offending. Typical of this position were the reactions of Mary McLure ('That's the biggest load of crap I've ever heard. I think politicians should get out in bloody society and have a real look at what's going on') and Donna Harrison ('It's bullshit').

Some parents were more relaxed about the difficulties of bringing up children. They conceded that there might be some justification in blaming parents, but they saw difficulties. Wendy Reynolds spoke from her own experience of being blamed for her son's offending.

> I'm in two minds about that. I agree to a point, but I don't agree in general. In general, I think most parents do the best they can and it's not the parents' fault. I don't think you can blame the parents totally for it. I think the parents do have a role to play in bringing them up and setting their values and everything, but just because you try and teach them doesn't necessarily mean the kids actually learn the values. I mean, I have totally different values to what my children are showing, and yet I've tried to teach them exactly the same values. So I find that comment really disturbing, actually. I mean, it's like saying children from wealthy families don't get in trouble and children from poor families do. You know, it's just not right.

When asked how she would reply to those who said to her that it was her fault her son offended, Wendy Reynolds replied:

> I have had that happen to me. My usual comeback is, 'Look, I've done the best I can and I've been to see so many different services and I've seen so many experts and they don't have the answers, so how on earth am I supposed to have the answers?' That's basically all I can say to them. I try my best. If they think they can do better, they can have them (Wendy Reynolds).

Other parents, while they, too, might agree with the media and politicians about the culpability of some parents, are sure they have done the right thing themselves.

> Not all families might be looking after them; my own family, I'm always here for them. I think the sons go out more than what the mum does. Mum's always home and I'm always here. That's what I said to them, 'You know, I can understand if I'm never home; or if there was no tucker (food) or if I'm drunk, or if people were coming all hours of the night drunk, I can understand that. But, I mean, I don't allow grog here (Josephine Heatley).

Interestingly, Aboriginal parents like Josephine Heatley, Ingrid Perkins, and Marie O'Connor, the grandmother of John, aged 11, saw their parental responsibility in providing a home and care for their children. Marie O'Connor, for example, said, 'I don't care what people think or the media think, I've always fed John, had clean clothes, and provided a roof over his head.' Ingrid Perkins felt that young people needed to discover their own ways of doing things. 'I don't think the parents are really to blame now, today. I just say we try our best, but after we carried them for a while, then they gotta do their own thing now. They got their own choice of minds, too, now. We can't force 'em to do anything that they don't want to do' (Ingrid Perkins).

In contrast to these Indigenous perspectives, non-Indigenous parents emphasized social control and family order. In addition, some non-Indigenous parents, while rejecting blame themselves, were quite willing to provide scapegoats outside the family for their children's offending. Some blamed the ineffectiveness of the wielders of social control in society, the police, social workers, and politicians. Kathy Fleming, for example, reproduced a commonplace discourse that laments the perceived loss of social control by state agencies.

> I've learnt in the last few years that most of these kids are from families that really do care about them and the problem is that they go to the police station or they go to a counselor and they're told, 'Oh, you poor child,' patted on the head and sent on their way to go and do it again. I'd like to see things get a lot tougher for these kids, and they be made to atone for what they do (Kathy Fleming, the coordinator of SNAP).

For other parents, the blame rests with the school system (Mary Smith) or other children who lead their own children astray (Ingrid Perkins) or the decline of Christianity (Donna Harrison). Some parents, again, blame laws that restrict the physical punishment that schools or parents can inflict on children. Once again, these parents' comments have a subtext of contemporary loss of control in contrast to a halcyon past where social and parental control was rigorous and enforceable.

> They should bring it back in that you are allowed to discipline your child, you are allowed to give them a good smack over the ear or a foot up the bum when they need it. And give the teachers back the responsibility of giving them the cane at school if they need it, and stop emphasizing how much rights the kids have. And giving the rights back to the parents of being able to discipline the child and

> know that you're not going to be taken to court for abuse or bashing them (Mary McLure).

A number of juvenile jurisdictions have implemented legislation that allows courts to fine parents for the offences of their children. Two parents felt that a fine would be counterproductive. (A $5000 fine on parents who failed to control their children was being proposed in Queensland during the time of this research). On the one hand, these parents said a large fine would not deter some offenders who would expect their parents to pay for any damage and, on the other hand, the threat of a large fine might mean that many more children would be made homeless as the parents got rid of troublesome children. None of the parents in this study approved of the idea. The bitterest response was from Ray Towner who worked with street kids.

> Oh, well, that's stupid. All you're going to end up with is 10,000 kids on the street because I know myself, that if my kid went out when he was 14 or something and stole or wrecked a house and I got charged $5000, I would throw him out on the street. I'd say get out there, go on, go out and earn the money the hard way. That's what will happen to all these kids. I could tell you that now. People on pensions or social security benefits, they're not going to pay it. What can they do? That is an insane idea of making the parents pay for it. When they first proposed that I laughed at them (Ray Towner).

While blaming parents for not controlling their children may be an evergreen political and media scapegoat, the parents in this study generally reject the suggestion that they are to blame for the offending of their children. The stories of their heartache at their children's delinquency, their attempts to understand and control their sons and daughters and the explanations that they give for their offending make a compelling argument for not blaming parents as a matter of course.

Conclusion

This chapter has addressed the issue of the causes of juvenile offending as seen by parents and juvenile offenders. Accounts by parents and children mirror the literature on juvenile offending and do not neatly dovetail into a simplistic explanation of 'the ultimate cause of juvenile crime.' Factors that parents identified as the causes of juvenile offending in their own children ranged the gamut from the intrapersonal to the family-functioning to environmental causes. The five children interviewed tended to lack stimulation in their own lives rather than see their offending as caused by internal problems.

Nor can this study be used to equate juvenile crime with the internal workings of family life. Only three families had multiple offenders in their family, and a number of offenders were determined to ensure that their smaller brothers and sisters did not follow in their footsteps. The families, then, were generally 'normal.' What was aberrant in them was not their criminality but the fact that they each had a criminal child.

If this is so, the campaigns by politicians and some sections of the media to scapegoat parents are unfair and unhelpful. Certainly, the parents in this study thought so, even if they also believed that there might be some parents who were blameworthy. Interestingly, a number of parents blamed themselves for their children's offending but vehemently denied that they were to blame in the terms that politicians were touting.

The next chapter will take the criminalization of families one step further. It will show how parents deal with state agencies when their children are charged and convicted of offenses.

Chapter Eight

Parents and the Police, Family Services and the Court

In addition to the effect that a child's offending has on the immediate family, there are other social relationships that have to be negotiated. There are the impacts on the wider family, the requirement to meet and deal with police and child welfare officials and to come to terms with the experience of the Children's Court. For parents, there is often the uncertainty of how to proceed in such circumstances.

This chapter will describe the experiences of parents seeking to confront the consequences of having a juvenile offender in the family. Parents noted the various ways in which they experience the intervention of state officials such as police, social workers and Children's Court officials. Overall, parents reported a sense of isolation, defeat and frustration. As will become clear, they felt that existing services focused narrowly, and ineffectively, on children's offending while neglecting the family context of juvenile offending.

Involvement with the police

The first parents may know of their child's offending is a call to them by the police to come to the police station because their child has been arrested. This news, especially initially, is often traumatic.

> I guess I was ashamed and embarrassed and felt pretty much alone because I didn't have my so-called husband there at the time to back me up. It was pretty harrowing because I didn't know what sort of reception I would get from them as to being told that I was a bad parent because my son had done this, or he'd behaved in this way, or

> he'd been stealing. And I just felt really uncomfortable and very uneasy when I first went up there to approach them and ask them, 'What do I do? How do I handle this. I need some help. I haven't got a husband here that's going to help me, can you help?' And to admit that, it really shook me up. I had a really good talk with the head of the Juvenile Aid Bureau and he couldn't have been nicer. He was really helpful and even made me feel at ease. He tried to make me feel as comfortable about doing it as possible (Mary McLure, mother of Cain, aged 17).

Parents have varying degrees and types of contact with the police, and this contact occurred within the parental home, at police stations, and at the Children's Court. Recurrent themes expressed by parents included the leniency of the system, the lack of consequences for the young person, the tardiness of police investigations and, for one parent, the feeling of violation after her house was searched.

Chris Watts discussed his experience with the police after John had been arrested for theft.

> Well, they did the arrest in front of us, except for the first time when we virtually got a phone call to say that he's down at the police station. And so we did the parental thing of going down and we got interviewed by the sergeant. And he was just very softly, softly. Now, John had been at the police station for more than two hours. And every time one of the policemen walked past him, he said, Son, you're going to go a row. We're going to get you for this. You've overstepped the line. And every policeman who walked past was ribbing him each time. And when I turned up there was no more of that. And also we walked straight into the sergeant's office and he virtually said, 'Listen, son, do you know the difference between right and wrong?' To which he said, 'Yes.' He said, 'Well, you're not going to do this again, are you?' And John said, 'No.' And he virtually said, 'Well, let's hope we don't see you again.' And that was the end of it.

Additionally, Chris Watts expressed his frustration about the lack of consequences for his son: John treated it as a joke. It was just a good thing for him to show off to his friends what he could do. However, Maggie Webb felt that the police had been very good to her.

> I would be asleep and a phone would ring at two o'clock in the morning. 'We've just arrested your son, would you like to come and sit in with him.' I've had the drug squad through the house. I've had a torch in my face at two o'clock in the morning and six policemen

through the house. You know, that is fairly traumatic, not that they weren't very good. They have been very, very caring and good to me (Maggie Webb).

Donna Towner had much the same experience of the police. A positive reaction to parents by police was given when police felt that parents were concerned about their children. Mrs Towner was portrayed as one of a minority of parents who cared about their children.

> I would have to say that the majority of the police officers that came here were very good. They were saying that it was good to see a parent that gave a damn and that there was so many parents out there that didn't give a damn. So on the few times he'd run away, I'd have to say they were pretty good.

On the other hand, Brenda Jones's experience was more intimidating than frustrating. She recounted her involvement with the police when her house was searched for drugs.

> Well, the night they walked in here with a search warrant and searched the place, it was absolutely terrifying and their attitude didn't help. They were very unsympathetic. They made me feel it was my fault and I was just as bad as he was. They don't make things easy. They're not nice about it at all. I suppose it's like a burglary, you know, they say you feel invaded. It was the same type of feeling that they'd come into my house for something that I hadn't done. You know, it doesn't make you feel good about anything.
>
> They just walked into the place and said, 'Here's a search warrant. We're looking for drugs.' And I said, 'Well, why?' And they said that somebody had told them. And then they got on the offensive, 'Well, we're coming in.' And I got really upset and I said that I was going to put in a complaint and later on they got my son downstairs and told him that if I put in a complaint they'd get him. They gave him the impression that if they had to frame him, they'd get him somehow or other. It was very frightening. There was no explanation. They just weren't very nice about anything.
>
> It made me feel that I was just as guilty as he was which was ridiculous, really, because I've never, ever seen marijuana let alone tried it. When I sat down and thought about it later, I thought it was pretty unfair because I'm not responsible for him using marijuana. It wasn't my fault he did it. I came from the era when you were brought up that the police were your friends and they were there to help, and then you get this attitude that everybody is guilty and they don't really care. To me they were very uncaring; we're going to do our job and it doesn't matter what the cost to whom. There was no

explanation to me about what was going on. It was just, 'You will bring your son in for a statement. You will do what we say,' as if I was as guilty as he was. And I think it's wrong. There was just no help. The attitude was, your son's a little criminal, no better.

If the police had sat down and said, 'This is what's going on. There's kids out there that are doing this and worse. Here are some places to contact.' Or even if they made the kids go and talk to somebody. It may not have helped, but it would have made me feel better. Possibly it might have helped him. I don't know. But, you know, if the kids had to do something rather than just go in and make a statement and get a smack on the wrist. I mean, okay, he was only 16, but he knew that he was doing the wrong thing. He knew it and he should have been held responsible in some way not just get a caution. So maybe if they were made to go and talk to somebody that knows what they're talking about. I'm not talking about counselors that come down on the side of kids, like most of them. I'm talking about people who can simply get down and say, 'Look this is what's going to happen to you if you keep on along this path.' It might get through to some of the kids, not all of them, but it might help some of them. And somebody to just sit there and say to the parents, 'You're not the only one. A lot of kids are doing this. And a lot of kids are worse.' That might help.

The degree and quality of involvement which parents had with the police coloured their opinions. Following extensive contact, Chris Watts was cynical and critical about the degree of police professionalism.

With police, senior police would say, 'It's not our problem. It's JAB (Juvenile Aid Bureau).' Basically when I had spoken to the police who'd rang up and say, 'Well, why didn't you do anything about it?' (They'd say), 'Well, it's not ours, it's Juvenile Aid Bureau.' They'd pass the buck as far as I was concerned. I think the police could be more decisive really, instead of mucking around on everything as far as kids are concerned. Rather than saying, 'Well, our hands are tied.'

Susan Watts was less critical of the police and saw the limitations of their powers. She recounted the following conversation. 'Well, one policewoman said to me, "All my job is I go out, pick them up, arrest them, send them to court. Pick them up, arrest them, send them to court."' This view on the part of police added to the Wattses' worries. Chris called the police 'gutless wonders' because they know the kids who are dealing drugs at schools and they are not doing anything about it. The sense of inactivity on the part of the police reinforced the feelings of helplessness that these parents felt about their son's offending. A similar sense of inaction by the police was voiced by Helen Joyce. Her daughter Amy, well-known in her neighbourhood for stealing, was threatened by vigilante groups. When Mrs Joyce was asked if she had reported the threats to the police, she replied that she had, but the police had not been helpful.

> I even reported to the police, but they knew what kind of record that Amy had, see. They didn't care; I reckon the police didn't care about Amy at that time because she was doing a lot of offending, see. Yeah. Well, I rang them up a lot of times. I asked them, you know, to help me look for Amy and there was always the excuse that we haven't got a car or anything. I was crying out for help, but no one wasn't given me any.

For the Watts and the Joyce families, the response they wanted from police was more than law enforcement. They seemed to want police to take on a disciplinary role as well. This was not something, as these stories illustrate, that police were able or inclined to do apart from some rather desultory threats to the young people to do better. The parents made the same type of criticisms of social workers and Family Services workers.

Contact with 'Family Services'

The Queensland Department of Families, Youth and Community Care (DFYCC), often known as 'Family Services,' has the statutory authority to enforce orders made by the Children's Court regarding the Juvenile Justice Act. Their key role is to supervise young people charged with offenses under the Act and monitor reporting requirements as determined by probation orders. Parents become involved with the Juvenile Justice Division of the Department as a result of their child's offending. Parents were also engaged with Family Services workers in aspects of case assessment and probation, and remained involved if the young person continued to offend.

Family Services workers undertake their work with juvenile offenders within a discursive climate in Townsville that is antithetical to their work. The criticisms of Juvenile Justice workers differ from those made of the police. As one editorial writer said, when defending parents for being not totally to blame for the crimes of their children,

> It is easier to take a holier-than-thou attitude to parents who do not seem to take responsibility for their children, but it must be remembered that there is an entire bureaucratic structure which militates against such responsibility. There is, as many parents will testify, so much interference from bureaucrats, social workers, counselors and others in the lives of families in Australia today that it is no wonder that some parents abrogate their responsibilities to them in defeat. (Editorial in the *Townsville Bulletin*, May 31, 1996)

When parents interacted with social workers and child welfare workers, they had one main criticism, the limited focus of the Department which offered services to the young person without providing any support to the parents or other family members. Parents saw this as workers taking the side of the offender against the parents. Jody Fraser notes,

> Family Services, they have all the support in the world and all the time for the kids that do offend, but they don't give the family a thought. Now, when I was talking to them after we got out of the court room, every time I said anything about myself or the other three children in the home environment, the response I got was how James was going to be affected by it, not how the other three children were going to be affected by it. You know, you've got the kid back and you've just got to deal with it. They don't ring you once a week and say, 'How are you going?' They speak to the kid that did it, and they believe what he's telling them. But they don't speak to you about it. You're made to feel like it's your fault. I feel that you're made to feel like you're responsible.

Many parents in this study, echoing media criticisms of Juvenile Justice workers, were like Brenda Jones, who felt that Juvenile Justice workers were lenient to the young people and dismissive of their parents.

> Well, I think the first thing that has got to be done is Family Services and all those services that are available to kids have got to stop coming down on the side of the kids and giving them a pat on the head and saying it's perfectly all right. The parents have to get some support. It's not the parents' fault, and I think these official people are going to have to start realizing that. The parents need help with these kids.

This sentiment was echoed by Susan Watts.

Their job is to be part of the Juvenile Justice and they just book him in. I would say that, even though they have spoken with us, it's always geared towards John. Obviously, their role is to be there for the child, and that's why they're called Juvenile Family Services (she means Juvenile Justice). But family means the whole of the family.

The views of parents indicated a sense of concern and urgency in attempting to deal with their children's offending. They were often frustrated by their own lack of success in putting an end to the young person's offending and by what they saw as the absence of services and skilled help in the community for parents. While, in the extract below, Donna Towner displays little knowledge of what Juvenile Justice workers do, some workers do not appear to make an effort to work together with the family and the offender.

> When we went to court, Family Services had someone sit in while we had the court session. We never had anyone come to the house. We weren't offered any help at all the first time we fronted up at court. The next time we fronted, they went in and sat again, nothing was offered again, no help, no counseling. When we went upstairs to the Magistrates Court, it was then that we asked for the curfew. They (the Family Services worker) were not for it and said, 'No you can't have it, if they break the curfew, it's another offense.' They weren't encouraging at all.
>
> Every time something's happened and I've picked up the phone and I've actually rung this department and spoken to the woman that's in charge of Brendan, I haven't had a good reaction as far as I'm concerned. We had an interview and she asked him what grade he'd gone to and he said, 'I went to Grade 9 (Freshman year) and she says, 'Oh, that's really good, isn't it.' And she swore, you know, there was 'effs' coming out of her mouth as she was speaking to me, and she was trying to get down onto Brendan's level and unfortunately I wasn't impressed. No, I'm not impressed with her at all.
>
> I thought that when the Family Services were appointed to oversee his twelve months probation, they would be coming out to the house to check on him. We haven't had one single, solitary visit. When he left home he didn't bother to let them know he'd moved and according to regulations he's got to let them know within three working days that he had moved. He's supposed to pay the consequences. He didn't. He's supposed to front up every Friday and see them and sign in and have an interview. He missed two weeks, she didn't even know. She did nothing, as far as I know. So I didn't feel she was doing the job that I thought the court meant for her to do.

Mrs Towner wants the Family Services worker to discipline her son, something that neither she nor her husband are able to do: 'I expected her to be on top of him, you know, to make sure that he was doing the right thing and, if he didn't, to jump on him and it's not happening.' Ray Towner thinks much the same.

> I don't think she's the right person for that kind of job. When the judge puts down orders that this had got to be done and so forth, and they totally ignore it, well there's something wrong, you know, within the system. So we're just not happy with them. They're just not doing their job, you know. I don't think they give two hoots about it really. As long as they're getting their weekly paycheck, that's it, you know. He (Brendan) needs somebody that's really strict on him and punishes him for doing the wrong thing, like he if he's supposed to turn up on Friday for his interview and he doesn't turn up, you know.
>
> Now, I was in a home about 30 years ago, right. I was in a home along with my brothers and sisters, there was eight of us, not because we'd done anything wrong but because we were living in poverty, and my parents couldn't kind of cope with it. I was the oldest, about eight years old and the youngest had just been born, and the Children's Services had no qualms about coming in. I was in there for five years, a good five years too, and . . .

His wife, Donna, interrupted at this point and noted, 'But the thing with that is, the family's still not together; they were never brought back together.' Unperturbed, Ray Towner continued,

> Now, we've still got the Family Services here, you know, and here's a bloke that's on 23 charges, has re-offended and all that and she's patting him on the back practically and they're doing nothing about it, you know. The whole world has gone to the shithouse, really, as far as I'm concerned.

Mrs Towner reiterated a common complaint of parents about all service providers in the area of Juvenile Justice, about the lack of support for parents. She also resented being patronized by the worker.

> There was no support, absolutely none. If I picked up the phone and said to her, 'He hasn't gone and done his community service today,' she'd say, 'Oh well, that's his decision.' And I didn't appreciate the way she swore when she spoke to me. She's sort of in a position of power when she's talking to me, and I felt as if she was talking down to me, maybe. I know I felt that when she spoke like that with Brendan perhaps she was trying to get down on his level and be his pal. There's no way she'd been my pal speaking like that. And she kept being positive about things, you know, like 'Oh, you went to grade 9. Oh, that's wonderful.' That's not wonderful. He hasn't done grade 10; he's not going to get a job. Who's going to employ him? And this stupid

woman is saying it's wonderful. She was being positive about things that weren't positive. You know, there's some things you can't be positive about and lack of education is one of them. Well, we're not happy with her anyway. We haven't had any dealings with anyone else.

Leaving aside the issue of the worker's inappropriate behaviour, there seemed to be an expectation from many of the parents, as the Towners have emphasized, that the Family Services workers would somehow be able to discipline the offenders and restore an equilibrium in the family that the parents sought but were unable to provide themselves. Helen Joyce had the same concern.

> I wasn't gettin' support and counseling. Aboriginal and Islander workers was coming around, but they didn't solve anything. So the problem was still there, it just kept on gettin' bigger and bigger until Amy got locked up a couple of times at Cleveland (a Juvenile detention facility). They wanted me to just discipline her and things but it's just that Amy wasn't listening to what we wanted her do, see.

Another Aboriginal parent voiced the same criticism. She compared the attitude of workers in today's Department to those of her youth, when Indigenous Australians were subject to strict and punitive laws that regulated every facet of their existence.

> Well, I wish Family Services would be harder on the kids. Like, I'm sick of Family Services saying, 'Oh, if Nicholas wants to go, he can go. But if he doesn't want to go, we're not going to force him.' No, I don't think that's wrong (to force him) because when we were small whatever Family Services said, that was that. If Family Services said, 'You go there,' you went. But now today, kids have got too much say about what they want to do. Like, Joe (the Family Services worker) said to me, 'Oh, if Nicholas doesn't want to go back (to school) they can't force him.' And I thought, 'Well, Joe, I really hoped you would force him to go.' I just sort of started feeling slack with the Department after that because I did want this kid to go to school (Josephine Heatley).

Parents often saw Family Services' workers in a policing role and were very disappointed with them when they did not enforce court orders or curtail the young person's offending. Many parents did not know what the workers were supposed to do and, despite having some contact with them, remained ignorant of their work and its limitations. Mary Smith, for example, was critical of the purely monitoring role that workers took with her son, Peter, aged 17.

> I thought that they could be more involved. I thought they could have come out to the home even and involve the parents more, but they didn't. (Peter) just had to go in, really, and sign the register. Every few weeks they'd do a review on him. So, you know, I was sort of disappointed that way. I think it might have helped if they came out and we sat down with my son and tried to work out some type of solutions to his behaviour and goals for him to achieve. I used to phone them quite frequently, you know, when he'd drive me crazy with his behaviour and they would offer advice over the phone. You found that sort of frustrating.

In the same way, Ingrid Perkins spoke about her lack of understanding of what Family Services' workers were supposed to do.

> Well, they just come around and put some rules down for him to abide by, you know. I suppose that's the job for what they do and I don't know what they supposed to do, see. I don't know how they gonna help, you know, they're just there. It's like they're there just because of the children who goes to court; then they got to keep an eye on them or something, I don't know. I can't see them helping me, helping him.
>
> You know, there are times when I wish they'd come to know a little bit more about him, why he's doing these things or if there's anybody out there who can help in some other areas, you know. I mean, really understand. I feel that I have tried doing my best, but I feel there are some other things that I want to know about, you know. I may be doin' something wrong, you know. I feel as if there is a lot of things goin' on in his mind but he don't want to talk to me about. He might want to talk to someone else about it. Yeah. I would like to talk to someone, sometime, maybe. But I feel sometime nobody has got time to talk. Yeah. I suppose they got a lot of other kids, too. I always think to myself, they must have a lot of other kids to worry about, you know. There's a lot of kids in trouble. Yeah.

When workers did intervene and try to change the young person's behaviour, some parents did not understand or agree with their methods. The Santorinis were critical of workers who tried to mitigate their son's offending. They wanted the worker to completely extinguish the offending behaviour of their son, Paul.

> The basic problem we had with Family Services was they turned around to us and they said, 'Right, he's committing three crimes a week now. If we can get that down to only two crimes a week, we're a great success.' That was their whole principle they operated on. Oh,

well, I felt like getting up and killing the lot of them. There's no use saying, well, only go out and do two a week. When you say no, you don't do any a week, that's it. Because all you're saying is it's totally all right for you to go and commit crimes. And they said no, that's the way we do it. We were really riled. I actually rang them up and abused them. I told them they were a bunch of idiots because if the kid is allowed to do two crimes a week, every week he'll just do two crimes and that will be it. They said, 'Well, yes, at least he's not doing three now. We're getting him, we're slowly weaning him off crime' (Daniel Santorini).

A further issue that reinforced some parents' beliefs that the Department was 'anti-parent' was the perceived lack of life experience and the relative youth of some Family Service workers. Parents spoke of their resentment about being told how to parent their child, especially when the worker was young. As Chris Watts said,

But with a lot of people in Family Services you get the feeling that they're only 21 or 22 years old as well, and you think, well, some of them don't look much older than 19. They're not much older than the kids who are offending.

Jody Fraser felt the same:

I found that I got very aggravated with some of the things that he (the worker) said to me. Now he, as far as I know, appears very young, is not married and has no children. I cannot stand it when somebody that has not been there and done it can sit there and tell you what you are and what you are not allowed to do. That really rubs me up.

In some parents' opinion, Family Services' workers seemed unable or unwilling to assist parents to come to terms with their children's offending. Chris Watts, in particular, found the Juvenile Justice workers to be dismissive of the Wattses' concerns.

We actually pleaded with them, 'Is there something else we can do?' We know he's not cured. We know that he's going to re-offend. What else can we do? And he (the worker) said, 'I've got an appointment that I've got to go to. I'm sorry, I really have to go.' And Susan had contact with the other worker a week later where we were told, 'Here's some places where you can get some counseling, but you can only go if John goes and if John agrees.'

While Brenda Jones did not have direct involvement with Family Services, her contact with other parents in a support group left her with a negative impression of that Department.

> Well, I think the first thing that has got to be done is (that) Family Services and all those services that are available to kids have got to stop coming down on the side of the kids and giving them a pat on the head and saying it's perfectly all right. The parents have to get some support. It's not the parents' fault, and I think these official people are going to have to start realizing that. The parents need help with these kids.

However, not all parents felt that workers ignored them or were incompetent. Angela Ralph learned from her 14-year-old daughter, Helen, that 'her probation officer was pretty good. She always was there for her appointments and that.' Josephine Heatley had great praise for a worker who had been involved with her son, Sam. '(Worker) came out straight away, you know, and he's a terrific guy. He's really helped me a lot with Sam and when he left I really missed him; he was always there. He'd come out and visit.' If there was one thing that parents appreciated in Family Services' workers, it was that they came and visited families at home. Even the Santorinis, who were aggressively critical of workers, appreciated when workers took the time to sit and talk with them about their child.

> The first one we had, she was excellent. She was actually making progress. Well, she was genuinely interested in Paul as a person. She didn't look upon Paul as just another kid. She was actually interested in Paul as a person; what we can do for Paul. She said, 'I'll get into trouble for it, but if ever there is any problem even after hours, here's my home number.' They're not supposed to do that. We're not supposed to know where they live. But her attitude was, well, kids are going to do things after hours. You can't say to people your caseworker is really working from eight to three, don't do anything after that. She said that she didn't believe in that. She believed that the kid's in trouble whether it's two o'clock in the morning, one o'clock in the afternoon; it didn't worry her (Jean Santorini).
>
> Her attitude was not the normal line that, you know, if he does three, get him down to two crimes. Her attitude was we've got to try and find a way to stop it. We've got to get him off this into something else. Well, we sat down and worked out things. We used to have talks for an hour or so. Half the time when the others would come around, they'd sit there for 15 or 20 minutes and say, 'Right, this is the form and this is what you're to do and how are you going to do this?' At least she would sit there and have a cup of tea and she'd talk about other things, not just the kid. She'd talk about 'how is family life?

What's so and so doing?' It was a genuine interest; whereas with the others it was just like filing a tax form. Terrible (Daniel Santorini).

In the main, parents had little idea of the work conditions and stresses that Family Services' workers bore. Mary Smith alluded to the high turnover of workers in her comments about a worker she thought was effective.

> I used to just ring them up all the time and talk to them, but, I mean, you know, there was such a big changeover there with the staff that were handling him. In the 12 months he was on the probation order, I think he saw about seven different people, so it wasn't very good that way. The last person he saw was really good. He was the only male that he had. He had him for the last couple of months. He was good because he took an interest in him, actually, and he said we've got to try and get you doing something, get you out there working or on a course. He said 'I'll take you to get your driving license' and organized for him to do a machinery course, that type of thing.

Overall, none of the parents had much sympathy or understanding of Family Services workers, although some parents got on well with individual workers. This lack of sympathy was in contrast to their attitude to the police, whom they generally thought were doing a thankless job. Parents expected more of Family Services workers than just monitoring offending and supervision of offenders. Some parents, such as Helen Joyce, expected support from them as well. 'See, the Family Service wasn't worryin' about how I was copin'. All they was thinkin' about is her offending and how we gonna' stop her from stealing. They didn't ask how I was feeling and how I was coping at that time. No. All they was worrying about is stop her from stealing. And they thought I was just fine.' While it is possible to get some inkling of what parents would like in the way of support and understanding from workers in their comments on the characteristics of 'good' workers already mentioned, one Indigenous Family Service worker was interviewed in conjunction with an interview with Helen Joyce. Mrs Joyce introduced the worker to the interviewer by saying, 'She's been a great help and support. She wasn't just workin' with Amy. When I had problems, I used to go cryin' to her and tellin' her and she always used to be there and she'll always listen to me. Yeah. And I could always open up to her.'

The Indigenous worker, when asked how she worked with Mrs Joyce, placed herself in solidarity with Mrs Joyce against non-Indigenous workers and noted that 'it's hard for our people to relate to someone (white) like yourself.' She took her stand as an Indigenous worker, with cultural knowledge and skills, in contrast to other workers who lack that knowledge and skill because they are not Indigenous.

> Oh, it's a cultural thing, I mean, we know how we can relate. We know how we can talk. We know how we can work things through and, you know, just the way we talk and open up to one another. I feel comfortable with Helen, and Helen feels comfortable with me. And Amy's the same because we've been able to relate really well.
>
> I think this is one of the things any Department has got to look at and especially when it's working with children; they've got to allow flexibility to work and support the family because if they're just going to go out and say, 'Oh, how are you going,' sign a paper, and take off, it doesn't work. There's a lot of things that the mothers got to have to be able to support the kids. Well, as Helen was saying, it (the non-Indigenous worker's focus) was all centred on Amy's offending, but they didn't stop to say, look at the real reason. That it's not only one person, it's a whole family environment. The family breakdown has to be addressed, you know. The only way to address that is not only to work with the child, but you've got to work with the mother, too, to meet the mother's needs to be able to cope. Departments have got to think about the family as a whole.

Helen Joyce joined in.

> There was other support workers, but they wasn't givin' us the support like Mrs (worker) was giving us. And she'll sit down and I'll offer her a cup of coffee and we can talk for hours if I got a problem. I shared all my problems with her.

Much of what this worker did focused on working with the family and especially establishing some form of structure to ensure the family looked after its members.

> I'll take Nancy to do the shopping and get all that over and done with. We try to organize outings as a family and that's happened. We've gone down to the swimming pool. Also we've seen a lot of family counseling. We all sit down and work things out what we've got to do and Helen is a lot stronger now. I suppose there's a lot of things that we sort of only focus on the here and now instead of looking at this one's future. But now we're focusing on that, and this is what I try and talk to Amy about all the time. Yesterday is gone, we can't do anything

about that. We got to start asking ourselves now for where you're gonna' go when you grow up. So it's dealing with education and living in harmony with mum and (stepfather) and the family. That's all fallen into place. A few little hiccups here and there, but nothing serious. As far as I know, Amy jumps on her bike and goes when she wants to go and that sort of thing, but everything is more stable, I think, than it's ever been.

This style of working is not confined to Indigenous workers. Wendy Reynolds had a similar story about a non-Indigenous worker. She only met this worker after many years of frustrating consultations about her son, Lester, aged 12.

> I went to a psychologist at Child Guidance. I went there for two years with Lester with his problems. We didn't even know that he had a problem at the time. We just knew that he was a difficult child, but they put it all down to bad parenting skills and blah, blah, blah. They more or less told me that it was all my fault. That made me feel very inadequate, but I felt really angry. I felt ashamed, yet the other side of me is going, 'It's not your fault. You've done the best you could.' So it's like fighting with yourself inside.
>
> Then I went to a pediatrician, because Lester was about eight at the time then, but I didn't want to let the pediatrician know that I'd been to Child Guidance because I wanted a separate, entirely different person's viewpoint. But he got out of me that I did go to Child Guidance, and he rang Child Guidance and Child Guidance told him that it was bad parenting, that I was just depressed and couldn't cope. And he told me there was nothing wrong with Lester, and I walked out of the office crying my eyes out; he made me feel so bad. So I didn't go to anyone for a long while after that.
>
> It was about two years ago that I contacted Family Services and told them that I wanted my son taken off me because I just couldn't cope with him any more. I was either going to kill him or he was going to kill one of us. And that was when they stepped in. They got us in contact with a social worker at Catholic Family Services and she worked wonders with our family. She was very, very good and I'm really disappointed that they've actually stopped the program that she was working with because it was wonderful, absolutely wonderful. She actually came to your house, gave you counseling—it wasn't like counseling it was like a friend popping in for coffee, you know. It was really good, and she would talk to Lance (Wendy's partner) and she'd talk to the kids and she'd take us out occasionally. You know it was just that you had someone there for questions and answers, and, basically, I think, that's the majority of the time is all you need, someone to talk to.

> It helped a lot because it was the reassurance that you weren't doing the wrong thing, that you were trying your best, that you were trying your hardest to cope with the way things are and to fix the way things are, and that's the best you could do so you shouldn't feel bad about it. I mean, she was wonderful. I really miss her. Her and I just clicked. It worked well (Wendy Reynolds).

There was a similar response from Flora Mackey, the mother of Matthew, aged 12.

> When they did actually send someone out, she was lovely. She loved Matthew to death, hey. He was a proper little shit to her, but she loved him to death. And they tried various workers with him, (but) they always ended up pissing off. I don't know whether it's just Matthew or whether they just get put on a new job or whatever, but the one that stuck with him the most would be Brian. Yeah. And he'll actually sit down and talk to Matthew and try and work out what's what; it's so hard. It's like trying to get into a jar of bees. You know.
>
> Most of the workers are very good. A couple of them were a bit stubborn with him because he bit back because he didn't want it first off. I don't need, you know, I don't need that. They talked with us as a family and sometimes they'd take Daniel and have a talk to him by himself away from the family (Flora Mackey).

A worker who can talk to and support parents, help them get organized, and listen to their problems is one that is valued by both Indigenous and non-Indigenous parents in this study. Workers who focused only on the offender or the young person's offenses were not seen as being 'good' workers. The lack of friendliness of workers to parents was mentioned a number of times. Parents saw this as either taking the side of their child against them or blaming them for the offenses of their child.

> On a hot day you can walk in there and you can feel the freezing cold. You'd think you walked into the Russian KGB. That's how cold it felt ... It always appeared as though Family Services Officers did not like being there. They were very cold and they weren't real friendly. 'Hello' and a false smile and that was about it and then we'll do this and this and this. It didn't feel like you were in there with someone wanting to help (Daniel Santorini).

The focus on the offending young person rather than on the young person within the family context, can have ridiculous consequences. Susan Watts was enraged when, on one occasion, her son John and Family Services and Court officials cooperated in a denial of her position and responsibility as a parent. John had been living with another family, had a falling out with them, and had attached himself to an Aboriginal woman who was attending court with other juvenile offenders.

> That was just ludicrous. The police served a warrant for John to appear. (The warrant was served) on the next door neighbour of the place where he was currently staying ... John had a falling out with her and she refused to attend. So he went up to the courthouse and linked himself to (an Aboriginal woman) because he was now 'black' and she was going to be his 'aunty.' She went into Court with him and the Judge heard the case. And he was given probation. I was furious. And I said, How can this happen? And they said that we just have to take what he says if he says he's living there and this is (his) custodial guardian (Susan Watts).

In this instance, the need of Court and other officials to process a case has taken precedence over the family context of the offending juvenile. In support of Susan Wattses' belief in the primacy of the family context, another parent, Kathy Fleming, mother of Natalie (17), argued the fundamental place of the family, over and above the interests of the actual offender, in dealing with offending children.

> A family is a unit and you've got to work together and unless you really look at that whole unit you just get nowhere, it just breaks down ... Yeah, I took Family Services to talk to her one day. I didn't get very far with it. That was just one in a long grind of the people that I went to. Very unpleasant because the focus was on my daughter because she was continually carrying on and when she had a good day the whole family had a good day. But when she had a bad day, heaven help the family, and you know that's not how a family should be, it shouldn't be focusing just on one person. (It should be) looking at what the family wants, not what the kid wants.
>
> I don't think that a lot of these social workers, unless they have lived with a kid like that, really have got any idea of what these families go through. It's okay reading a book about what this is about, but to actually live with it is something and that's really hard and I don't wish this on any parent. (They need to) be more open-minded; they seem very closed to what parents have to say. It's just the impression that you get when you talk to them (Kathy Fleming).

Another point of contention with some parents is that their knowledge is not valued by workers. Helen Joyce was very distressed at the placement of her daughter, Amy, in a remote

Aboriginal community. She knew the danger she would be in and was very upset when she was proved right.

> I told Family Services, I said don't send her. I wanted them to lock her up anywhere. I got a feeling like she was gonna' get raped again, but they wouldn't listen, so they sent her anyway. The Family Service man used to go there and he didn't know what was goin' on. Every time I saw him he used to say Amy's all right. But I see from the photos that he took that she was stoned and they couldn't see it, she was right out of her face on marijuana. And she used to ring home constantly, 'Mummy, I want to come back home.' And deep down in my heart I knew something was wrong and I reported it to the Family Services. All they could say to me was, 'Oh, that's just her way of getting back here so she can offend again.' They was worryin' about her offending. But I knew there was something more than that.
>
> I went there, I wanted to do my own investigation and find out what was really wrong. I heard that all these boys were having sex with her, all these girls (were) pushing her to have sex with all these boys for drugs and they were bashing her up. In one part she was walking around with a black eye. She was all busted up and had all these bites all over her neck, love bites (hickeys). Family Services said it would have been a safe place because I got relatives there, but none of my family would look after her for me because they're all alcoholics, too, see. And it just got worse until one of the Christian ladies there told me, you gotta' get your daughter away. Then as soon as we got back, a week after, she was doin' the same thing, offending again.

It appears from this account that Mrs Joyce and the worker had a different agenda for Amy's placement. For the worker, the removal of Amy from Townsville to a remote community and the subsequent cessation of her offending was the primary purpose of her placement. Her re-offending, when she returned to Townsville, justified this stance. The worker had also followed Departmental guidelines that emphasized that Aboriginal children should be placed with relatives, wherever possible. For Mrs Joyce, though, the worker focused on Juvenile Justice concerns and on a narrow view of what was good for Amy rather than relying on her knowledge of the actual situation. She was saying that the worker had not taken family context and family knowledge into consideration.

Another family, the Santorinis, were also critical of workers who made decisions without tapping into parents' knowledge.

> So they felt that he was safer with his sister than us. But they didn't look at the other person that his sister was with at the time. The worst thing is they put him in the care of two people who were living in a two-man tent in a caravan park and he (the sister's boyfriend) was a drug user. But he was a lot better there than he was in our home (said sarcastically). I was angry (Jean Santorini).

It becomes clear in these accounts of worker/parent interaction that there is little communication and understanding of each other's position. Parents are often critical of Family Services' workers because they are too rushed, too impersonal, and too ready to take the offender's side, which parents interpret as being against them. Parents have little understanding of the demands of working with juvenile offenders and seem to expect that workers will be able to discipline young people that they have been unable to discipline for some time.

At the same time, some parents identified characteristics of 'good' workers that they valued. These included a certain genuineness on the part of workers toward parents, the ability of workers to understand the offending within a family context and not just as an individualized case, and an appreciation of those workers who attempted to curtail offending behaviour rather than just monitor it. Part of working within a family context was the valuing of parents' knowledge of their children and of what might or might not work with offenders.

Going to Court

All the parents in this study had had experience of the Children's Court. 'It was traumatic enough to be there with your son in that situation. It's not a nice situation to be in to start with, let alone with what goes on top of that' (Maggie Webb). Initially, part of that experience was the strangeness of the Court and the guilt many parents felt in being there with their children.

> Those people always stare. (I was) frightened and scared inside because I didn't know if it was just me and Amy against everybody, you know, because there (were) just (the) two of us . . . I could see it on their face, why can't you control your daughter, where's the discipline? I could just feel it. I sensed it (Helen Joyce).

Flora Mackey finds Children's Court 'scary. I hate going to court.' The first time she went to Court and found out that her 12-year-old son Matthew had 20 charges of breaking and entering and stealing from houses, she said,

> Oh, I nearly wet myself. They reeled off about 20 charges and my jaw just dropped and I'm standing there going, 'Oh, he didn't do it.' It's going through my head and I'm thinking he couldn't have done this. There's no way he could've done this, hey. And they're going blah, blah, blah, all these addresses and I'm just standing there. I think I just went into shock. I just stood there and thought, Oh, no. I got to the stage where I refused to go to court. I couldn't handle it.

Ingrid Perkins, too, was fearful of her first visit to Court with her son, Robert.

> I was scared. I'd never been in a court before. I didn't know what was gonna' happen, you know. But after a while it's just like another part of my home. I've just been in and out, in and out. I just go in and sit down and listen and go out again, you know. The Aboriginal Legal Aid people are there to let us know what to expect; like he might get sentenced or they might just let him off for, you know, probation and things like that.

Maggie Webb's son, Carl, appreciated that his mother came to Court with him, 'although he used to say to me, I don't care if you're not there.' She added, 'I always went. I don't think I missed one because I felt that if you're not there that means you don't care what happens. And I do care.'

On a dissenting note, Josephine Heatley realized that the Court reflected and reproduced the same racist behaviours as the wider society. 'Well, I don't like the court. The court is where all the black kids are left last and all the white kids go first. When Sam first started getting into trouble, well, I was always up there early sitting, sitting, sitting and realized then, 'Oh, all the white kids get dealt with first and all the black kids gotta go last.' So I don't rush up there anymore now since I know the procedures.' Nevertheless, for Wendy Reynolds, when her 12-year-old son, Lester, first went to Court, the experience helped to reduce her anxiety. 'Actually, I thought it was a relief. It's very weird because I thought, well, this is it, he's now going to court and he may understand now that this is not a game and this is getting serious. And he did. He stayed out of trouble for a good 12 months.' Children's Courts are places where parents are silenced and made to feel the power of the law: 'Everyone feels like when they're in court, that's the authority up there and you're the person down there and you behave and this is all' (Wendy Reynolds). Yet, Susan Watts was unimpressed by the manner of court proceedings. 'You go into this little separate room where (the Magistrate) sits up and he's got his little clerk that's taking all the notes. And the policemen just sit there and don't even look at you . . .. The Judge asks, "And who is with you today?" and "Is this your mother?" Then he sometimes says hello to you and that sort of thing. And then you don't speak.' Mrs Watts found the ritual of the Court both exasperating and silencing. She spoke of her observations of the duty solicitor (attorney). 'The actual duty solicitor speaks to you for five seconds and jots down a few pointers he might be able to use and he stands up and says, "This boy who." . . . He makes out he's known him for 100 years. [And the solicitor says], "he is a student at this school and this is his first offense, or second offense, and he's seen the errors of his ways."'

Despite Helen Joyce's fear that the Court would think she was to blame for her daughter's offenses, other parents did not feel the same pressure. Ingrid Perkins was pleased to note that the Court put responsibility for offending with the offender: 'They just always tell him that it's his choice now. They don't put that blame on to me, you know. I feel all right when I go up to the court now to listen because it's up to him to do what they tell him to do or else he's going to get into trouble. I try to tell him what's right from wrong, you know, and that's all I can do.'

Nor did Wendy Reynolds feel that the Court officials blamed her.

> No, I don't feel that I'm on trial because they make it known that it's not your mother's fault. They're very good in court that way. They say, 'Your mother and father have done their best,' they emphasize that it's not the parent's fault. Well, in my particular case anyway, they never, ever made me feel like it was my fault. They made him (Lester, aged 12) feel like he's letting us down, that he's got to get himself straightened out. All I can say is that I never felt like I was on trial.

Despite this positive feeling for parents in the Townsville Children's Court, many parents were exasperated with the procedures and the sentencing. Again, some parents wanted the Court to undertake the control of their children that they had been unable to exercise. Sentencing in the Children's Court was seen by some parents as a soft option for juvenile offenders. As Susan Watts stated, 'I've been to Court with him heaps of times, and it's a social affair. This juvenile system cracks me up. They (the offenders) all stand outside and laugh and joke . . . . And then they go inside and then it's even bigger jokes when they come out and they only got a warning. The Judge says to them each and every time when they give these warnings, "Next time you're going to go (to the Detention Center)". But next time they don't.' The Santorinis had fostered street kids so they were well aware, and bitingly cynical, about what would happen to their son, Paul, when he came to Court.

> Oh, we knew exactly what they were going to do. The Judge was going to turn around and say to him, right, behave yourself, don't do it again (Daniel Santorini).
>
> See, because we've both been there with the street kids as well beforehand. So that's why we knew how the court system worked. We were quite disgusted, actually, because we used to go there with the kids from the street-kids farm, and you'd have kids actually standing outside there bragging with each other saying, oh, such and such a Judge is on today, this is a piece of cake. I don't know about Daniel, but that used to rile me. I used to think that was bad. You know, the kids were actually going to court and making a joke of it. To me that was wrong. So, basically, when we went there with Paul we knew the same thing would happen (Jean Santorini).

For Donna Towner, the perceived leniency of the Courts is a direct affront to parental and social control of young people. She appeared to be as hard on her own son as she would be on any offender.

> If you do something you're not supposed to do, there's a consequence and you have to face that consequence and that's not happening. Okay, fine he (Brendan, age 15) only busted a water sprinkler, but he still broke his probation and the judge said to us when we were in court that he would only have to spit on the sidewalk and they would call him back and he'd get another, harsher penalty. That didn't happen.
>
> He went to Children's Court and got 20 hours community service. The community service does nothing for the people that they've offended against. It doesn't replace broken car windows, smashed windows, graffited buildings, and stolen goods. They should have to work for those people in some way. Kids have to learn that society's

not going to cop it. You know, if they're not prepared to listen to their parents, which most of them aren't, then they have to learn that society is not going to cop it and they're going to be accountable for their actions and not their parents (Donna Towner).

Conclusion

In addition to having an offending child, parents, as part of the process of criminalization, must confront police, Juvenile Justice workers and Children's Court magistrates and officials. Most of the time, parents look to these workers to provide support for their parenting and for the imposition of social control to replace the loss of parental control. They became upset, angry and frustrated when these workers did not perform the services the parents expected. Most opprobrium was vented on Family Service social workers and child welfare workers, especially when their actions were seen as supporting the offender against the parents. Similarly, some parents found great difficulty with the perceived leniency of the Children's Court sentencing. These parents reacted negatively to young offenders' apparent disdain for the legal system.

However, there were workers who were able to support parents and, at the same time, in the opinion of parents, provide appropriate services to the offenders. These workers were highly praised and highly valued. What characterized the practice of these workers was the ability to treat parents as parents and not as criminal accomplices. Spending time with parents and other members of the family showed a commitment by these workers to a family-centred practice that parents valued. Yet, virtually no parents were mindful of the possible stressful and demanding work of Juvenile Justice workers. In the parents' narratives, workers, good or bad, did not appear as flesh and blood people, but merely as supports or hindrances in the parents' battles with their children.

Chapter Nine

Making Parents Pay: Parental Restitution

In Britain, the United States, and Australia, there has been a shift to what might be called 'punitive individualism.' This holds that the individual is directly responsible for his or her own actions and should therefore be held accountable (and punishable) for criminal behaviour (Hudson 1996). In an effort to 'get tough' on juvenile crime and to placate growing 'public concern,' governments have introduced a range of legislative measures designed to extend and strengthen sentencing options available to the court. While such legislation has been directed mainly towards the sentencing of offenders, the notion of responsibility extends to the role played by parents in the control and supervision of their children.

In Britain, Australia, and the United States, parental restitution has been used by the courts as a means of punishing parents for the criminal actions of their children, thereby extending the boundaries of culpability to include the family as a whole. In so doing the legislation necessarily absolves the State from any direct or indirect responsibility for generating the conditions that might lead to crime and instead places the blame squarely on the shoulders of young people and their parents (Cook 1997). In this sense, parental restitution constitutes a formal recognition by the legal and judicial systems that the neglectful actions of parents have contributed directly to the irresponsible behaviours of their children.

The rhetoric of making parents pay

During the course of this research, the Queensland State Government, as have other governments, sought to implement new measures to reduce juvenile crime and the causes of crime. Parents and their offending children were targeted by the then Queensland Attorney General, Denver Beanland, when he commented that this important legislation would bring responsibility on both the offenders and their parents. The community has had enough (*Townsville Bulletin*, May 30, 1996). Another local newspaper editorialized,

> Parents in Townsville and Thuringowa may find themselves in the dock alongside juvenile offenders under new laws announced last week. And they may also have to pay up to $5000 compensation where courts decide it is appropriate for crimes committed by a child. Attorney General Denver Beanland on Wednesday launched the start of a four-week consultation period for amendments to the *Juvenile Justice Act* 1992. These changes are tough, yet fair, Mr Beanland said. (*Townsville Sun*, June 5, 1996)

All Australian states and territories have legislative provisions that enable courts to order parents to make restitution for the crimes of their children. In Queensland, where the research for this book took place, provision for parental restitution in cases of juvenile crime has long been part of the State's legislative framework. Thus, section 62 of the *Children's Services Act 1965* states that restitution or compensation could be imposed on parents or guardians where a failure to exercise adequate care, supervision and guardianship could be demonstrated by the court. The *Juvenile Justice Act 1992* includes similar provisions, although it is more concerned with the principle of 'willful neglect' of parents in relation to cases of juvenile crime. Like the previous legislation, the *Juvenile Justice Act 1992* asserts a clear causative link between the negligent actions of parents and guardians and the offending behaviours of their children. Section 197 of that Act states: 'If it appears to a court that finds a child guilty of an offence relating to property or against the person of another, on evidence admitted or submissions made in the case against the child—that willful failure on the part of a parent of the child to exercise proper care of, or supervision over, the child was likely to have substantially contributed to the commission of the offence then.' The Act thus implicates parents (under the principle of 'willful failure') in the instigation, if not the commission, of their children's offending behaviour. However, the

Act offers no clear definition as to what might constitute 'willful failure' on the part of parents and guardians in cases of juvenile crime, or how a 'substantial contribution' to the commission of the criminal act might be assessed. In allowing for such a broad framework of interpretation, the Act opens up the possibility for considerable variation in decision-making by the court. The Act further states that parents may be required to pay compensation to victims for damage, loss, or injury resulting from the criminal actions of their children.

The Act also involves parents and guardians directly in the court process by enabling them to contest the imposition of restitution orders. Thus, section 197 of the *Juvenile Justice Act 1992* states that parents may be required to 'show cause, as directed by the court, why (they) should not pay compensation.' Mindful of the fact that some parents may find it extremely difficult to meet restitution or compensation payments, the Act provides for consideration of financial circumstances of 'the parents' capacity to pay the amount, which must include an assessment of the effect any order would have on the parents' capacity to provide for dependents' (section 198).

Other Australian states and territories have similar provisions. In New South Wales, the focus of the *Children's (Parental Responsibility) Act 1994* is on parental responsibilities as they relate to the criminal actions of young people. The Act's major concern is with penalties that may be imposed by the court on those parents who have, through willful action, contributed to their children's offending. Thus, the Act states that:

> A parent who, by *willful default or by neglecting to exercise proper care and guardianship of the child, has contributed to the commission of an offence of which the child has been found guilty, is guilty of an offence.*
> (section 9. Our emphasis)

The New South Wales legislation states explicitly that willful failure on the part of the parent in the child's offense is, in itself, an *offense*. This formally extends the boundaries of culpability from the child to include his or her parents or guardians. Moreover, like the Queensland legislation, the *Children's (Parental Responsibility) Act* allows for the possibility of parents to face further criminal proceedings should they breach the conditions of the court order.

Similarly, the Tasmanian *Child Welfare Act 1960* ratified in the *Statute Law Revision (Penalties) Act 1994* states in section 25: 'A parent or guardian of a child who, by willful default or by neglecting to exercise proper care and guardianship of the child, has contributed to the commission of an offence of which that child has been found guilty, is himself (sic) guilty of an offence.' The Western Australian *Young Offenders Act 1994* provides for restitution orders to be imposed on offenders in respect of loss or damage experienced by victims (section 56). Section 58 states that in the event of a young person failing to pay a sum for restitution or compensation the court may require a responsible adult to pay: 'An order for any payment by the young person may be accompanied by an order that, in default of payment by the young person, the payment be made by a person specified in the order who is a responsible adult.' Parents and guardians are further involved in compliance of court orders by the requirement to give security for the good behaviour of the young person. In the event that an order is breached or where the offender fails to attend the parent may be required to offer an explanation to the court (section 58). In effect, therefore, parents and guardians are directly implicated in the regulation and accountability of court orders in respect of their children.

An interesting variation to the principle of parental responsibility is contained in the Northern Territory's *Juvenile Justice Act 1984*. Parents may be required to pay restitution or compensation for loss and damage experienced by the victim (section 55). Although no specific reference is made to parental restitution, the ceiling of $5000 in respect of restitution by the juvenile offender would suggest the possibility that families are ultimately required to raise such sums. Parents may also be required to pay a proportion of the costs associated with having a young person in a detention center: 'Where . . . a juvenile is ordered by the court to be detained at a detention centre, the court may . . . order that a parent or the parents of the juvenile pay an amount towards the cost of detaining the juvenile in the detention centre, which amount shall not exceed $100 per week, for each week during which the juvenile is detained in the detention centre' (section 55). This provision is to be used by the court in cases where 'it is satisfied that the parent has or the parents have, as the case may be, *failed to exercise reasonable supervision and control of the juvenile*' (section 55. Our emphasis). Clearly, this provision is in keeping with the principle of parental restitution, although in this case, the beneficiary is the Northern Territory Government. In effect, those parents deemed to be negligent in terms of care and control are penalized for the misdemeanors of their children. Moreover, the fact that parental contributions towards the cost of a detention center placement are an order of the court means that failure to comply may result in further penalties being imposed (section 55).

In the United States, the proposition that some parents should be held responsible for the criminal actions of their children has been widely accepted by a number of state legislatures. One of the first states to make the explicit link between children's crimes and parental supervision was California. The *Parental Responsibility Act 1988* made parents criminally liable for failing to supervise their offending children adequately. Culpable action on the part of parents in respect of their children's offending could result in imprisonment of up to one year or a maximum fine of $2500.

Although the law was challenged by various legal and welfare organizations on the grounds that it was subjective and an intrusion into the privacy of family life, the Californian Supreme Court upheld the law (Yea 1997: 1). Since 1988, at least 17 other states have passed laws that hold parents criminally responsible for the crimes of their children. States have also strengthened provisions that allow courts to pay the cost incurred by courts or the corrections system in dealing with their children. Arizona, Alaska, Idaho, Dakota, New Hampshire, and Virginia have passed laws that make the parents of offenders responsible for victim restitution. In Kentucky, parents may further be required to meet the adjudication costs incurred by their children's appearance in court (Yea 1997: 1).

The growing emphasis given to parental responsibility in respect of juvenile crime in the United States has found expression in a number of celebrated court cases. For example, in a recent case in Indiana, the parents of a repeat juvenile offender were fined $30,341 for the cost of incarcerating their son. While the judge in the case stated that the parents were not held responsible for their son's crimes, their actions had nevertheless led to his offending. As the judge stated, 'The effect is to make parents aware of their responsibility for their children. They can't pass it off to some social agency. That's a smokescreen' (Collins 1990: 21). One of the underlying messages associated with a number of the laws that seek to penalize parents is that the contemporary family is, for a host of reasons, ill equipped to care for its children. As a senior representative of the National Center for Juvenile Justice stated, 'We want them (parents) to be something they used to be, but the mechanism is gone. The father is not always the breadwinner, and the mother is not home nurturing. That's all gone' (Collins 1990: 34). A somewhat different view was aired in the wake of another celebrated judgment in which the parents of a Detroit teenager offender were each fined $100 and ordered to pay $1,000 court costs for their failure to properly supervise their son. A spokesperson for the American Civil Liberties Union not only questioned the constitutional basis of the parental responsibility laws but also pointed out that the fining or jailing of parents would do little to address the particular skills required of a parent, especially when confronted with a son or daughter who offends (Meredith 1996). Moreover, writing in the influential *Stanford Law and Policy Review*, Howard Davidson (1996: 28) argues that, 'It is simply inappropriate to rush into legislative solutions that punish parents for their children's criminal acts without ensuring that effective services are readily available to families at all income levels ... to help them to be better parents.'

Internationally, the increased emphasis on penalizing the parents of juvenile offenders has received support from those seeking a tougher approach to law and order and condemned by those who see such developments as worsening the plight of many already hard-pressed families. Notwithstanding the latter, it appears from the move toward parental responsibility in legislation and judicial action that the link between parental supervision and juvenile crime has now become an axiomatic feature of many criminal justice systems.

In Britain the recent focus on the family as the chief cause of delinquent behaviour occurred during the premiership of

Margaret Thatcher during the 1980s (Pitts 1988). Growing concern over rising juvenile crime and outbursts of violent inner city disturbances led to calls for tougher law and order measures aimed at punishing offenders and their apparently negligent parents. Indeed, the links drawn between poor parental supervision and juvenile crime led to specific provisions in two major pieces of legislation designed to combat growing levels of lawlessness among the young. The *Criminal Justice Act 1991* stated that in cases where a young person under the age of 16 has been convicted of an offense, the parents should be bound over to exercise 'proper' care and control of him (sic) (*Criminal Justice Act 1991*, cited in Halsbury's Statutes: 707). Parents are bound over for a sum of money up to £1000 which is to be forfeited if the child re-offends. Although the Act required the consent of parents in order to impose bindover orders, refusal to accept such an order could be met by a fine! In fact, therefore, parents were given little choice. The second major piece of legislation (this time passed under the conservative administration of John Major) was the *Criminal Justice and Public Order Act 1994*. The Act built on the 1991 legislation by requiring parents who are bound over to ensure that the child complies with the sentence of the court. Under the Act, parents would be required to forfeit their monies if the child failed to meet the conditions of an order, let alone if the adolescent re-offended.

The Conservative government appeared bent on using fines against parents as a major strategy in its war against the rising tide of juvenile crime. Shortly before its eventual loss in the 1997 General Election, the Conservative government was deliberating on more penalties that could be imposed on the parents of juvenile offenders. In a Green paper entitled *Preventing Children Offending*, the government set out a range of proposals aimed at penalizing the parents of juvenile offenders. Child Crime Teams made up of social workers, teachers and probation officers would apply early intervention strategies aimed at supporting at-risk young people and their families. The teams would be backed up by hard-hitting and punitive parental control orders which would require parents to ensure that their children were at home during certain hours or attending school. Parents could also be required to pay reparation to victims for damage inflicted by their children. Parents failing to comply could be penalized in several ways, including fines up to £1000, probation orders, confiscation of driving licenses and, in more extreme cases, curfews and electronic tagging (*The Guardian*, March 5, 1997).

The election of New Labour in June, 1997, meant a continuation rather than reform of many of the previous government's law and order policies. Indeed, a discussion paper published shortly before the election noted the central importance of the family and styles of parental supervision in the creation of crime and delinquency among the young. Drawing on a number of criminological studies of offenders, the authors concluded that, 'The evidence is now strong that the character of parental supervision in the preteen years holds the key to later delinquency. This raises the question about whether as a matter of public policy there should be more intervention in the upbringing of some children' (Straw and Anderson 1996: 5). Despite the uncritical acceptance of 'the evidence' and general avoidance of the many social and economic factors bearing down on the families of juvenile offenders, the authors proceeded to discuss a range of policy proposals aimed at ensuring parental compliance in the upbringing of law-abiding children. Central to these were Parental Responsibility Orders which were aimed at those parents who 'have not been prepared to accept guidance and counseling to help them cope with their behaviour.' The order would require parents to attend counseling or guidance sessions. 'They [parents] would learn . . . how to set and enforce consistent standards of behaviour and how to respond more effectively to challenging adolescent demands' (Straw and Anderson 1996: 18). The discussion paper does not specify the particular range of penalties that would ensue if parents failed to comply with such requirements.

Despite the changed emphasis in the proposed policies from 'control' to 'responsibility,' it is clearly evident that, like Australia and the United States, the British approach to juvenile justice has embraced the central idea that 'the family,' as the main instigator of 'antisocial' behaviours, requires punitive legislation to ensure parental compliance in the crusade against crime.

Families' experiences of restitution proceedings

Despite the rhetoric about parental responsibility, in Queensland, at least, courts have been reluctant to order parents to pay restitution. Our research found only seven instances of parents in North Queensland being asked to show cause why they should not be required to pay restitution for their children's offending. We were able to interview four of the seven parents. Three of the four parents had been ordered by a magistrate to show cause when, in 1996, the then Queensland Attorney General was in Townsville and talking tough about juvenile crime and parental responsibility. This instance, reported in the *Townsville Bulletin* under the headline 'Juvenile Act Trialled,' noted that a Townsville Magistrate was requiring three parents to appear in court 'to argue why they should not pay for the crimes committed by their children' (*Townsville Bulletin*, May 30, 1996).

The three boys involved were John Watts, Carl Webb, and Richard Marcos. As John's mother remembers,

> They had stolen the cars and taken them for joy rides, and then returned to the place of their next car and the boys were sort of caught in the act after one car exploded in flames and they were seen walking away. During the Children's Court hearing, the magistrate decided that he would ask us to show cause and we were told by him to obtain legal counsel. There was myself and another family, we went and obtained solicitors and the third family also got a barrister. And then their barrister and solicitor approached my solicitor as to whether I would share the cost of the barrister for the appearance in court because it was really quite costly. I think my share of his fee was like $300.00. John was pleading guilty.

Interestingly, when interviewed, Mrs Watts had a copy of the *Juvenile Justice Act 1992*, from which she read:

> It says, 'Section 197 permits a court which finds a child guilty of certain offenses of his own initiative or an application by the prosecution to decide to call upon a parent to show cause why the parent should not pay compensation. The court may do so if it appears to the court that the willful failure on the part of the parent of a child to exercise proper care of or supervision over the child is likely to have substantially contributed to the commission of the offense.' I mean, at this time we had been involved with Family Services (DFYCC) for quite a period of time asking for help, telling them our situation, what problems we were having, and then to be asked this

> sort of stuff. So I went to my solicitor and gave him John's background and also what attempts we'd made to do something about correcting his behaviour, etc., and so forth.
>
> When we went back to court, the barrister baffled the magistrate, well, not really, he just went on, you know how barristers always talk in mumbo-jumbo language? Mumbo-jumbo language about the legality of how the summonses and things were served and why was one partner served and not the other partner and all this sort of stuff. And at some point not so far past that, (while the barrister) was still going on about this and other things, the magistrate then withdrew the charges without even hearing them. So the show-cause thing was then thrown out. $600 later we don't get proved guilty or innocent.
>
> The reason the magistrate said that he gave for withdrawing the charges or dropping the matter or putting it aside, or whatever they call it, was that he had subsequently, and why he didn't get his facts right in the first place, read the report from Family Services (DFYCC) which indicated to him that he was barking up the wrong tree, obviously.

Carl Webb's mother was one of the other parents at the court on that day.

> At that time that we went to court with the children to be sentenced, the magistrate read out the law which I believe had only just been passed. We were all there; there was myself, one of the other boy's mother and the grandma, and then the other boy's mother and father. So there were five of us. Five adults, I believe, in the court. And the magistrate said that this law had been passed, and he felt that we would be charged because the children had caused a fair bit of damage and costs. I don't deny that, but I was a bit taken aback because as I said at the time, he wasn't living under my roof. I was, well, a little bit taken aback because I really didn't know what would happen. It wasn't until afterwards when I got home and I started to think about, well, what could I have done to have prevented or tried to stop what was going on. I couldn't (have prevented it) because he wasn't here for me to have any control over.

Mrs Webb was shocked at being asked to show cause. She found the accusation unfair and the process unfair and expensive.

> If I'd been a different type of personality, I would say I probably would have had a nervous breakdown. But I'm a fairly stoic sort of personality and I just had to take it day by day. I think the biggest kick in the butt from all that was that I needed to get a lawyer to prove my innocence from what (the magistrate) had charged me with and from the fact that he charged me, not my husband as well was, I felt, a bit unfair because, even though he didn't live at home most of the time

Making Parents Pay: Parental Restitution

he still was a part of the family. He still was aware of what everything that was going on. I mean, I speak to him at least twice a week by telephone. He was aware of what was going on.

I had to get a solicitor to defend myself because we weren't financially poor enough to get Legal Aid. There was myself and one of the other mums. She actually went to a different lawyer. Then the two lawyers conversed with each other, and then they both got a barrister to defend the things. My court costs were $2,500 which was a large whack out of our pocket at the time. The other girl, I believe, she was charged $800, so she must have had a better lawyer or a lawyer that was perhaps a little bit less greedy or what, I don't know. But that in turn put lots of extra pressures on the family.

Mrs Marcos, the mother of Richard, was the third parent in the court that day. She, too, felt it was unfair of the magistrate to ask the parents to show cause. 'Yes, that was my first time, you know (in court). Ever since in my life that's the first time I experienced going to the court. Yeah. So I was nervous and all that, you know. I'm really nervous.' Mr and Mrs Marcos had a solicitor from Legal Aid because they could not afford to employ one. Mrs Marcos went on to say,

It was unfair for us. Yeah, it is unfair for us that time. Yeah. Because you know, as I said, as a parent we had nothing to do with it, you know, got nothing to do with it because we have raised him in a good manner to respect others, that's what always I've told him. That is our house rule here at home. But his behaviour we cannot do anything about. Yeah.

When the three families came back to court to 'prove their innocence' in Mrs Webb's terms, the magistrate did not proceed.

Because then after that, they just threw it out of court anyway because the lawyer said that virtually the magistrate had to prove that we were unfit parents, you know. Now, that's a very hard thing to do. Um, so it was just quashed. Nothing was proceeded with. But then I felt that I had been wronged and I felt angry at the system to be even charged with it. So I said to my lawyer, 'What recourse have I got to do that?' In fact, it cost me a lot more than just $2000. That was just the one lump sum. It cost me, I reckon, in other follow-up fees probably another $500 or $600 on top of that. And I said to him, 'What recourse have I got to recoup,' because I felt that it was unjust that I should have to pay that sort of money just to get somebody up there to say that I was innocent because as far as I was concerned I should not have been charged with it to start with. Because if (the magistrate) had done his homework properly, you know, he would have realized that Richard's address was not my address.

Mrs Watts is very cynical about why the three families were asked to show cause. She says they had no warning that this might happen.

> I'd been quite a few times (in court) prior to that and now heaps more times after that and never been asked to show cause again. I think it must have just been politically in the air at the time. They were discussing this in the media and probably in Parliament and the magistrate thought, 'Oh, well, we might give this a little bit of a run,' not forgetting how much it was going to cost ordinary working people, and there's no provision in the Juvenile Justice Act to award costs in court.

Mrs Webb has much the same suspicions.

> It was just like, oh, wow, this is something new. This might be something I could use to prove a point or whatever. I don't know . . . so I still feel bitter about that. Certainly I wasn't prepared for it. I mean, I was prepared to see the worst for my child. I certainly wasn't prepared for anything for myself to be charged. I mean, that was, that was a shock. And, you know, at the time, I mean, my husband wasn't home. I mean, I really didn't know where to proceed.

Surprisingly, both John Watts's and Richard Webb's mothers agree that some parents should be made to pay restitution for the crimes of their children. Mrs Watts says it depends on the situation but 'I'm sure that there's cases where the parents should be asked to.' Richard Webb's mother thinks much the same.

> In certain circumstances, if a parent can be proven to be neglectful and bring up the child to steal and rob—I mean, there are parents I dare say that bring their children up because they do it themselves—in those circumstances, I think the parent should be accountable because then the child sees no differently, you know, if dad can do it, then why can't I?
>
> But, at the same time, it's very difficult because if a child does commit a crime, as in burn down somebody's house, how do you then say, 'Well, yes, that's going to be the responsibility of the parent to pay that.' I mean, you can't do that. I think (restitution) should be in community service. It's very difficult to put a money thing on it. But, I still think that the community does lose out by parents that are not doing the right thing. They should be brought to somebody's attention to try and help (them). If they can't help the parent, well then the child should then be given some sort of support.

Making Parents Pay: Parental Restitution

The members of the Ryan family, who were also interviewed in regard to parental restitution, have an interesting story to tell. The Ryans are an Aboriginal family whose son, Luke, had been breaking into houses and stealing. Eventually, the Children's Court magistrate decided that Luke's parents should be made to pay $2,500 as restitution for their son's offenses. Unlike the previous families, they were not told in court but received a letter in the mail demanding payment. They took the letter to the Legal Aid solicitor who said, 'Don't take any notice of it because Matthew's a juvenile. But when he turns 18, if they'd like to get it back, they can.'

> Oh, we were panicking, hey? And then, that's when we went and seen a solicitor again, and he said, 'Don't take any notice of it. And that was the first time we heard about that when we got the letter from the court. He (the magistrate) never told us face to face in court.' We were at home one day and that's when that letter came. Oh, it sickened us. Where were we going to get two and a half grand, you know, just like that by a certain period of time. We thought it was a joke. You know, true. Well, that was our first impression, you know. We said, 'No, this can't be right. No way in the world, because they never said anything at the court about it, you know, and we were always there. Always.
>
> That's what I mean, it come as a complete surprise, you know. It come out of the blue. Like, you know, the police prosecutor or even the Magistrate, he never come up to us there and said, 'Oh, Mr and Mrs Ryan, you'll be getting something in the mail soon.'

Of further interest, after the letter had been sent, one of the DFYCC officers came to the Ryans' house to ask about their assets. One can't help feeling it was a scheme devised by court and welfare officials, outside court, to make the parents pay for the offenses of their child. Mrs Ryan was angry at the whole episode.'To tell you the truth, I felt pissed off. You know, I was looking at the system and said, 'Oh, you know, you can't come back to the parents then surely?' Even Luke said, 'Never mind, mum, I'll go to work and I'll get a job, I promise, I'll pay it all back.' He was panicking then because he realized what was happening, you know. He got a bit upset, too, when he seen all that.'

Why restitution proceedings do not work

In general, the principle of parental responsibility is now firmly established in juvenile justice systems. However, the introduction of penalties for parents has attracted considerable criticism from various legal and welfare organizations. Generally, such criticism is directed at the assumptions that parental neglect is a direct and major factor in the occurrence of juvenile crime and that restitution is an effective means of dealing with juvenile crime. In relation to the former, the Australian Association of Social Workers (AASW) notes that : 'The assumption that a parent can guarantee a child's behaviour at all times is simplistic, and is likely to affect disproportionate numbers of those on low incomes who are least able to pay fines. Convicting parents for not exercising proper care transforms failure as a parent into a crime, and punishes parents without offering help' (AASW 1995: 1). Similarly, the Australian Catholic Prison Ministry and the Church Network for Youth Justice (1996: 4) point out that parental restitution is likely to '. . . further alienate families who are most in need of support and encouragement. . ..' In a similar vein, the NSW Council of Social Service (NCOSS) notes of the *Children (Parental Responsibility) Act* that, '. . . the impact on families already under stress is unimaginable in practical (financial) terms but is also likely to be considerable in terms of already fragile intra-family relationships' (NCOSS 1995: 8).

In Queensland, proposals to make parents liable for up to $5000 restitution in cases of property damage caused by juveniles have been condemned by a number of key justice organizations in the state. Thus, the Brisbane Aboriginal Legal Service, Youth Advocacy Centre, Queensland Council for Civil Liberties and the Victims of Crime are united in their opposition to parental restitution, principally on the grounds that it is likely to make the plight of many already hard-pressed families considerably worse (*Courier Mail* May 3, 1996). An editorial in the *Townsville Bulletin*— a regional paper not noted for its liberal stance on juvenile crime— pointed out that the newly proposed penalties in Queensland might be applied differentially to offenders' parents: 'The proposal that parents be required to pay up to $5000 for their offspring's errant ways is . . . flawed. For a start it would seem that only the parents of means will be required to pay. Those well off financially will go scot free' (*Townsville Bulletin* July 3, 1996). As one Australian commentator noted, 'it has been pointed out that rather than dealing with the issue of crime informally at a local level, the imposition of 'external solutions' is likely to bring more juveniles (and their parents) into contact with the justice and welfare systems' (O'Connor 1992: 329).

In Britain, restitution provisions, although appealing to law and order lobbyists, came under sustained attack from a range of legal and welfare organizations. Referring to the 1991 legislation, the editorial of a Magistrates Association's magazine noted that the government's proposals for bindover orders would '. . . damage such little cohesion as already may survive in already fraught and vulnerable families' (cited by the Penal Affairs Consortium 1995: 3). Even sections of the conservative press pointed to the shortsighted nature of the government's proposals. Thus, an editorial in *The Times* of November 10, 1990 stated that 'Bind overs make perfect sense to middle class ministers, who generally leave the learning of adolescence to their children's boarding schools. For, say, the single mother in Brixton, struggling against the odds to keep a young person on track, they represent only a threat. Many such parents will be tempted to wash their hands of their responsibilities.' The Penal Affairs Consortium—an umbrella organization for a wide range of justice agencies in Britain, concluded that 'An emphasis on fining and binding over parents is likely to produce injustice, to place struggling families under even greater stress and to increase rather than reduce the problems which promote delinquency' (1995: 4). Similarly, in a review of the governments measures in respect of families, criminologist, Dee Cook, notes that 'Not only are such [measures] doomed to failure, they have negative social consequences too— the likelihood of increased youth homelessness and a deepening of poverty—should already poor parents be financially penalized for their children's offending' (Cook 1997: 145). As already noted above, similar criticisms of parental penalty have been expressed in the United States where such measures have long been intrinsic to juvenile justice systems. As in other countries, critics of parental penalty argue that such measures are likely to add significantly to problems already besetting families.

The four case studies detailed in this chapter show that not only that the courts appear somewhat reluctant to evoke parental penalty in cases of juvenile offending, but also that parents themselves see very little ameliorative value in such measures. In Queensland, there appear to be a number of reasons for this, not the least of which is that it may be difficult to prove that parents are contributing to the delinquency of their children. Certainly, this seems to have been the case for the Watts, Webb, and Marcos families. In the Ryan's case, the situation suggests an attempt by officials to coerce an Indigenous family into paying restitution without going through the due process of the law. Moreover, taken alongside the accounts of parents in earlier chapters, the findings suggest that parental penalty constitutes something of a crude judicial response to many of the complex problems facing families, particularly those trying to grapple with the problems of a son or daughter offending. It is difficult to see, even with the most generous eye of punitive responses to law and order, how parental penalty can contribute in any meaningful way to preventing further offending. While such measures may placate those who locate the causes of crime in the context of family dysfunction or of simple parental neglect, they do little in a practical sense to support parents attempting to deal with an offending child in their midst.

Conclusion

Legislative provision for parental penalty has been a prominent feature of western systems of juvenile justice over recent years. The idea that parents should be held responsible for the offenses of their children has found its way into the statute books of countries such as Australia, Britain, and the United States. Much criticism has been levelled at such measures by a range of social and welfare organizations and, not least, by parents at the receiving end of the justice process. Such criticism casts serious doubt on whether parental penalty can be effective in preventing further offending among juveniles; indeed, it is more likely to create new problems such as increased family tensions (possibly resulting in youth homelessness) and financial hardship. It does little or nothing to help and support those parents who, despite their own efforts, have not succeeded in preventing the offending of their children. Parental restitution also tends to individualize the supposed causes of crime by taking attention away from the social origins of offending and rather heaping the blame (and responsibility) upon the shoulders of children and their parents. In so doing, of course, crime becomes transformed into a simple moral or skills issue that is strikingly consistent with many of the individualistic explanations of offending currently in public circulation.

CHAPTER 10

Learning Some Lessons

This book has told the stories of 20 families whose children were caught up in the system of juvenile justice in a north Australian city. We began the book by noting the trend in recent years to blame the parents of offending children for their children's crimes or for not controlling their children. We also contested some of the more simplistic parent-blaming ideas that permeate current discourses on juvenile crime and showed that some parents were trying to curb their children's negative behaviour. Furthermore, we criticized the flaws in research dealing with families and crime on its often erroneous assumption that the families of those labeled as juvenile offenders are demonstrably different from other law-abiding households.

The emphasis given to the term responsibility and its application to areas of social policy (including crime control) is one of the most revealing trends in recent years. The term has been applied in two distinct ways to the area of families and juvenile justice. First, there is the effort to coerce parents into crime management through the legislative provision of parental restitution. Second, there is the co-option of the family into the crime control culture via crime prevention projects, family group conferencing, community panels, and the like. In each of these initiatives, heavy emphasis is given to the notion of responsibility, and parents are compelled through fear of penalty or through moral obligation to participate in the culture of crime control.

While it would be disingenuous to see all such initiatives as simply the machinations of an oppressive state, the reliance on notions of personal responsibility and accountability in relation to offenders and their families reveals a system of justice based on narrow and morally charged understandings of the origins of crime. The fact that family responsibility is talked about so often and with such moral opprobrium tends to assume that families have passively abnegated their supervisory duties. This, of course, is a gross misreading of the impact of crime on families. Even in the most disorganized and crime-prone communities, continuing efforts have been made by residents to assert their own forms of crime control. Externally coercive approaches that emphasize family-based crime management fail to recognize the efforts which parents go to, not only to deal with the offending of a child, but also to manage the consequences for the family as a whole. It is all too easy to regard parental failure as the main cause of juvenile crime. Much of the law and order rhetoric is underpinned by the assumption, repeatedly conveyed by politicians and the media, that the family is the formative crucible of offending behaviour.

The problem with simplistic explanations of juvenile crime is that they invariably gloss over the social and political contexts of family relationships and ignore many issues—poverty, status, lack of human and material resources—experienced by families in increasingly divided societies. It has been well established that juvenile crime is closely connected to issues of poverty and disadvantage (Youth Justice Coalition 1990). This is not to suggest a direct causal relationship between low income and crime (Smith 1996) or between unemployment and crime (Bessant 1996a); a small number of the families in this study came from relatively financially secure backgrounds. However, factors such as poverty and unemployment have some bearing on the choices that young people make in shaping the course of their lives (Pitts 1990).

Structural inequalities are also closely linked to the processes of governance in the liberal state (Bessant, Sercombe, and Watts 1998). Indeed, the way society is organized in terms of its policing determines which social groups end up in the criminal justice system (Hudson 1993). In Australia, for example, Aboriginal young people are vastly overrepresented in the Australian criminal justice system, as are non-Indigenous young people from poor and disadvantaged backgrounds (Beresford and Omaji 1996). Social and political contexts may explain why certain young people are more likely to be charged with crimes, but these contexts do not determine that parents' social or economic backgrounds are a cause of young people's offending. In addition, while penalties imposed on parents may assuage the uninformed concerns of those who see crime as merely the result of parental or family failure, penalties alone do nothing to assist those families faced with the care and supervision of an offending child. Family responsibility, always the moral catch-cry of conservative commentators, has over recent years changed considerably from the simple exercise of adequate care and control over children. In areas such as health, education, and crime, family responsibility has figured prominently in social policy directives to devolve more and more communal functions once assumed by the state back to the family.

This notion of responsibility has taken on a highly individualistic meaning and the systematic rise of parental restitution legislation across a number of countries, as well as allied measures aimed at increasing family involvement in the crime control culture, are reflective of a changing ideological climate. While family-centred initiatives aimed at improving the supervisory and caring skills of parents may provide some improvement in the communication and caring practices of parents, they are inadequate without a full appreciation of the impact of poverty and 'other external stresses which diminish the quality of life' (Utting 1994: 20). The coercive nature of current approaches to crime control has ensured that it is the perceived failure of parents to exercise adequate supervision that is now widely regarded as the major cause of rising juvenile crime. In the United States, Britain, and Australia, parents may now be prosecuted for the misdemeanors of their children, thereby buttressing the popular idea that crime is essentially a by-product of the negligent family-household. However, it is not just any parents: it is those parents from the errant underclass, the urban poor, black, and sole-parent households who are most often held up as the new criminogenic pariahs of western societies. A convenient way of explaining the actions of such families is not to dwell on unemployment, poor housing, lack of family support, or diminishing welfare provision, but rather to point to moral aberration or lack of parenting skill as the cause of crime. The inference, therefore, is that offending results from a failure of parents to act responsibly.

The purpose of a book to record the accounts of parents about their children's offending was to illustrate some of the complexities faced by families in such situations. The accounts of parents presented in previous chapters suggest that far from being indifferent to the actions of their children, parents seek desperately to find ways out of their predicament. They are often surprised, shocked, and angered by what they consider to be the unacceptable behaviours of their children. Their attempts to explain the onset of juvenile crime, and to do something about it, are indicative of the active ways in which families attempt to manage their children's offending. While parents' accounts varied, there was agreement that parents were never less than traumatized by their experiences of formal justice. Indeed, in some cases, the intervention of police officers, child welfare workers, and court personnel were devastating for parents who felt isolated, humiliated, and exposed to a system they really did not understand or welcome. The criminal justice system was a strange, amorphous world of individuals and professional groups who frequently displayed ignorance of the feelings of parents and, surprisingly or not, often lacked a capacity to curtail a young person's offending behaviour.

Given the efforts to which parents in this study went to curtail their children's behaviours, it would seem ludicrous to blame them for a lack of responsibility. Some may indeed have been better than others at enforcing the rules and sanctions of the household, and some were occasionally successful in putting an end to their son's or daughter's offending. Generally, however, few outright claims of success were manifest in this study. Success may simply have meant keeping a son's or daughter's offending behaviour down to a bare minimum, or achieving partial compliance with household rules.

Families and juvenile crime

Unsurprisingly, having a child who is continually offending is a traumatic and unnerving experience for parents and families. In contrast to the opinions of some commentators who imply parental indifference or collusion, Susan and Chris Watts's reactions are typical of the parents in this study. Their emotions went from shock to dismay, anger, frustration, and resignation. They were actively involved in efforts to deal with and put a stop to their son's offending. They supported him when he went to court and visited him when he was in prison. They have not given up on him, although they are the first to admit they do not know what else to do. Similarly, other parents in this study contradict popular assumptions that they are uncaring and irresponsible. Their children's offending had an adverse effect on them and their families.

When parents try to explain offending behaviour they mirror the complexity evident in the literature on the causes of juvenile crime. Some children have been disruptive all their lives, others appear to have had some sort of catalytic experience that has tipped them over into offending. Some explanations emphasize psychological causes for offending, others emphasize the functioning or lack of functioning of the family. Some parents cite external traumas or circumstances such as ineffectual control in society by police, social workers, and politicians. While there is nothing new in the reasons parents gave for offending, one interesting finding is that the five offenders interviewed had much more mundane explanations for their own and others' offending. The main reasons they put forward to explain their offending were boredom and excitement. Of the young people, only Robert Perkins (poverty) and John Watts (loneliness) were able to explain their offending in terms other than self-centred behaviour. According to the five young people interviewed, the causal issue seemed to be lack of stimulation in their lives rather than internal psychological problems. While the young people's explanations need to be tested against their family's judgments of their situation, the realization that young offenders may positively view their offending as self-actualization necessitates a response from law enforcement agencies that is congruent with young peoples' aspirations for personal agency. As Pitts (1990: 36) has noted, 'offending is a way, albeit often inadequate and self-defeating, of solving problems.'

In regard to blaming parents and families for juvenile offending, the campaigns by politicians and some sections of the media to scapegoat parents is unfair and unhelpful. Certainly, the parents in this study thought so, even if they also believed that there might be some parents who were blameworthy. While a number of parents may have blamed themselves for their children's offending, worrying whether they had done enough or too much for their children, they were adamant that they were not to blame in the terms that politicians were touting. Nor can some parents' acceptance of blame be used to equate juvenile crime with dysfunctional family life. Only three of the 20 families interviewed had multiple offenders in their family and a number of offenders were determined to ensure that their smaller brothers and sisters did not follow in their footsteps. The families in this study, then, were not producing juvenile criminals but were rather families with a juvenile offender among their children.

One startling contrast in the study was between those parents who emphasized punishment, control, and a focus on young offenders to compel them to be more responsible and other, particularly Indigenous, parents who emphasized acceptance, communication, and developing self-responsibility in their children. Parents who attended the Tough Love group SNAP found this a source of support for themselves but still had to deal with their offending children. These parents, often isolated before joining the group, tended to focus their anger and hurt on professional workers, who, they felt, were too lenient on their children. Other parents, especially Indigenous parents, rejected the hardline attitude of the SNAP group. They tended to receive support from churches or family or felt that keeping the lines of communication open with their offending child was the best way of dealing with the offending. The differences between the two groups of parents can be summarized in the contrast between the more closed, controlling families and those that appeared more open and communicative with their children. The latter may well have placed controls on what their child could or could not do, but did not appear to be as rigid as the Tough Love families.

Finally, as the chapter on restitution showed, it may be difficult to prove legally that parents are contributing to the delinquency of their children. Taken alongside the accounts of parents in other chapters, the findings suggest that penalizing parents is a crude response to the complex problems facing families, particularly those trying to grapple with the problems of a son or daughter offending. The idea that parents should be held responsible for the offenses of their children has been rejected by the four sets of parents in this study who have experienced it. Their criticism casts serious doubt on whether parental penalty can be effective in preventing further offending among juveniles; indeed, it is more likely to create new problems such as increased family tensions (possibly resulting in youth homelessness) and financial hardship. It is difficult to see how punishing parents can contribute in any meaningful way to preventing further juvenile offending. While such measures may placate those who locate the causes of crime in the context of family dysfunction or of simple parental neglect, they do little in a practical sense to support parents attempting to deal with an offending child.

The call for tougher penalties and increased policing may in fact contribute to the growth of criminalized populations (Hogg and Brown 1998). Generally, tough laws and order measures do little or nothing to address the complex problems facing young people and their families. Such measures may in fact worsen the social exclusion, isolation and marginalization experienced by growing numbers of young people (Finer and Ellis 1998). Penalties imposed on the parents of juvenile offenders may also worsen the plight of many already hard-pressed families, thereby ensuring an increase in the very conditions that may give rise to crime (Cook 1997).

Professional responses to families and juvenile crime

Initially, parents looked to police, social workers, and Children's Court officials to provide support for their parenting and for the imposition of social controls to curb offending. Interestingly, their concerns are similar to a UK report (NACRO 1994: 4) which cites six key areas where parents could be encouraged to play a more significant role when juveniles are arrested. The six areas are

i. at the point of arrest;
ii. when decisions are being made whether to caution or prosecute a young person and whether to offer additional support services to the young person and the family;
iii. while a young person is remanded on bail or as part of a bail support program;
iv. at court;
v. during the administration of supervision orders, intermediate treatment and specified activity orders and other community-based programs for young offenders;
vi. when a young person is either remanded or sentenced to a period in prison custody, or secure accommodation.

Parents in this study became upset, angry, and frustrated when the police, the court, and child welfare workers did not perform the services the parents expected. For a couple of families, the response they wanted from police was for the police to take on a disciplinary role in regard to their children. This was not something that police were able or inclined to do apart from some rather desultory threats to the young people to do better. Some parents, too, had great difficulty with the perceived leniency of Children's Court sentencing and reacted negatively to young offenders' apparent disdain for the legal system. In this, they were echoing widely held beliefs about the inadequacies of juvenile law enforcement (McMahon 1997) and reinforcing punitive practices to restrict young offenders' legal rights (Pitts 1990).

The fiercest parental criticism was of Family Services social workers and child welfare workers, especially when their actions were perceived as supporting the offender against the parents. In many accounts in this study, there appeared to be little understanding of parents' positions by workers. The focus of attention on the offender as an individual and not within the family context was not appreciated by parents, who showed anger and puzzlement at what they saw as an undermining of their parental roles. The lack of friendliness of some workers to parents was seen as either joining with their child against them or blaming parents for the offenses of the child. It seems that workers who fail to understand the trauma parents go through, or who dismiss their concerns, are sabotaging relationships within the family and, in parents' eyes, possibly reinforcing the negative behaviour of the children. Alarmingly, the exclusive focus on the offender by some workers seemed to imply that they believed that intervention at the individual level could be successful in spite of their ignoring the family context within which that individual lived. A worker who focused only on the offender or the offenses was not seen by parents as being a good worker.

Further criticisms of Family Services' workers by parents arose because of the way they carried out their work. When workers were too rushed and too impersonal, parents interpreted this as a further positioning of workers against them. Parents have little understanding of the demands of juvenile justice work or of the number of cases workers have responsibility for. Virtually no parents were mindful of the possibly stressful and demanding work of Juvenile Justice workers. Nor were parents mindful of the pressures placed on workers by lack of resources and staff. In the parents' narratives, workers, good or bad, did not appear as flesh and blood people, but merely as supports or hindrances in the parents' battles with their children. Some parents also expected workers to be able to discipline young people that they themselves had been unable to discipline for some time. Unrealistic expectations of workers' capacities and coercive powers led parents to harsh criticisms of workers, sometimes blaming them for the continued offending of their children.

However, it needs to be emphasized that there were Juvenile Justice workers who were able to counsel and support parents and, in the opinion of parents, provide appropriate services to the offenders. These workers were highly praised and highly valued. What characterized the practice of these workers was their ability to treat parents as parents and not as criminal accomplices. Spending time with parents and other members of the family showed a commitment by these workers to a family-centred practice that parents valued. A worker, then, who can talk to parents, support them, help them get organized, and listen to their problems is one that is valued by both Indigenous and non-Indigenous parents in this study.

The characteristics of good workers, in parents' terms, included a certain genuineness on the part of workers toward parents, the ability of workers to understand the offending within a family context and not just as an individualized case, and an attempt to curtail offending behaviour, rather than just monitor it. Part of working within a family context was the valuing of parents' knowledge of their children and of what might or might not work with offenders. For those who work with the families of juvenile offenders, it is important to steer away from easy explanations of offending. We argue that workers need a comprehensive understanding of the wider contexts that affect offenders and their families. Workers also need to recognize the fact that families are complex social entities, each with its own way of communicating. Building relationships with such families requires a considerable amount of sensitivity and skill and an understanding of the issues these families face in an increasingly difficult world. Workers need to acknowledge these difficulties in an open and respectful way and give due regard to the efforts parents may already have attempted in dealing with a child's offending. Without such an approach, workers are likely to be viewed as useless or counterproductive.

This argument for cooperation between parents and workers should not be taken for a positioning of all young offenders as merely misguided souls. To caricature criminalization simply as the end product of repressive governance may be as unhelpful to these families as blaming them for their own misfortune. Juvenile crime, whatever its causes, is a harsh reality that also affects the lives of others. It is with this thought in mind that certain family-based initiatives may be of direct and practical assistance in helping to curb the excesses of some young people. An example of one such initiative is found in a support group established for the parents of young offenders in a northern English city (Horwath and Griggs 1989). The group was formed in recognition of the requests for help and support made by the parents of repeat juvenile offenders. Like the parents in this study, the English parents said that they were 'always on trial,' one mother saying that the idea 'that you have failed is always pushed on you.' Every effort was made to guarantee confidentiality and to avoid labeling or stigmatizing the participants. Parents were invited to attend the group on a voluntary basis. Discussions were conducted on a wide range of topics connected to their children's offending. The evidence suggests that participants benefited enormously from the group both in terms of the reduced sense of isolation (experienced also by many parents in this study) and the knowledge gained of how to build more constructive relationships with their children. The group leaders commented that 'none of the parents felt labeled because of attending the group. They had done it out of feeling isolated and facing criticism and lack of understanding from people who knew of their son's offending' (Horwath and Griggs 1989: 23).

Another project, Parents Against Crime, this time based in London, included a number of programs and activities aimed at engaging parents in discussions of their children's offending. Workshops, seminars, individual counseling, support groups, and a national telephone help-line were set up to assist parents in coming to terms with their children's behaviours and to facilitate a better understanding of parenting skills. The parents reportedly benefited greatly from simply talking to others about their problems (De Souza 1994). Many similar statutory and nonstatutory projects now operate in Britain, Australia, and the United States. Although often focused on parents to the exclusion of the family as a whole, these projects offer a way for parents to reflect on managing their children's behaviours. In Britain, a recent Home Office report on families and crime urged the government to establish open access family centers that could be used by the community to support those families having difficulties with their children (Graham and Bowling 1996). Such centers, if run on an open, noncoercive basis, could provide an extremely useful source of help and support to many beleaguered families. In Queensland, Australia, the state department responsible for administering juvenile justice has recently established Juvenile Justice Centers for serious and recidivist offenders. Located in high crime communities, these centers may also offer some much needed help to the families of juvenile offenders (even though the court order compelling offenders to attend suggests a strong degree of coercion) (DFYCC 1998a). The same state department has issued an extremely useful booklet for parents of juvenile offenders. Written with a considerable degree of sensitivity, the booklet offers some practical advice about what parents can do when a child offends. Called 'If Your Child Breaks the Law' (DFYCC 1998b), the booklet suggests ways in which parents can address the problem of offending through better communication with their children, as well as seeking help for other related matters from accredited agencies.

Families, crime, and social responsibility

The responsibility for the problems besetting families are certainly not all of their own making. Thus, it may be necessary to take a panoramic look at the quality of life in our neighborhoods and communities. Indeed, as pointed out by the National Council for the International Year of the Family, responsibility for family affairs (including the prevention of crime) is not simply a matter for parents alone.

> All social groups and individuals share responsibility for the living standards and quality of life of families . . . It should be stressed that if access to jobs, adequate income, appropriate and affordable housing, health and community services and to adequate transport is limited, this is most likely to be a failure of public policy not of individual families and their members. (National Council for the International Year of the Family 1994: 12)

At the macro level, workers may also assist families in a way that is less oriented towards intrafamily issues and aimed more at addressing factors such as unemployment, poverty, housing, and the lack of recreational facilities and support services. This approach means that the worker's assessment of the family situation must adopt a more community-oriented perspective that is cognizant of the way in which external forces shape the day-to-day realities of family life. The distribution of benefits and burdens across society should alert us to the way certain populations are seemingly more favoured than others. The issues of crime and crime management may necessitate a closer examination of the big questions associated with social inequality and its relationship to crime (Cohen 1985). This may mean taking a more expansive community-centred view of practice than the traditional reliance on aspects of casework (Ife 1997), moving away from individualistic intervention to a practice approach that addresses factors such as poverty, unemployment, disadvantage, and social exclusion (Holman 1995). As the secretary of the Townsville Victims of Crime Association emphasized during the research for this study, 'We have to address the whole problem. We have to address why kids get involved in it, what we can do as a community to prevent it, what sort of action the [city] council, the State Government, even the Federal Government can do to ensure that the juveniles don't continue to create this violent society' (*Townsville Bulletin* May 31, 1996). Individualistic renditions of responsibility are ultimately unhelpful in addressing all the complexities associated with juvenile offending. Parents are caught up not only in intrafamilial issues, but they are also subject to the vagaries of external forces such as unemployment, material hardship, lack of support services and so forth. At a time when poverty is increasing in western countries and when welfare budgets are being systematically eroded by governments, it is likely that external factors will bear down ever more severely on families. One of the most worrying developments over recent years has been the growth of social inequality in western countries and the tendency of government to introduce harsher law and order measures. The inverse relationship between expenditure on welfare and on law and order (with the latter increasing) suggests some serious transformations in the way in which western governments are responding to social problems (Chomsky 1996). Nowhere is this more evident than in relation to young people and families.

The victim-blaming discourse of recent times tends to avoid any conception of collective or state responsibility for problems besetting families (Jamrozik and Sweeney 1996). As Hartley and Woolcott point out, a balance should be struck between the responsibilities of the state and the wider community, and the private concerns of the family: 'Responsibility for individuals in society is approached between the state, the community, families, and individuals. In relation to young people and families, the crucial issues are the circumstances under which the main responsibility lies with the family, the young person, or with the state, and the most effective balance between private and public support.' Despite the need for such balance, recent policy relating to responsibility for young people 'has reflected a general move toward the family taking more responsibility' (Hartley and Woolcott 1994: 37). This is particularly the case in respect of crime control, where governments have increasingly pointed the finger of blame at families rather than acknowledging the constraints placed upon them through governmental neglect (Campbell 1994).

CONCLUSION

To date, empirical research into the families of juvenile offenders has been driven by the aim of identifying factors that lead to delinquency. Accordingly, the family is seen as the essential site for the production of deviance. Despite an abundance of research, there is little evidence to support a simple or unilinear link between particular family characteristics and juvenile crime. In any event, this way of thinking about crime and its causes fails to address why some young offenders and their families (rather than others) find themselves embroiled in the justice system. By giving voice to parents, this study begins to question the simplistic representations of the family that often features in research literature on juvenile offenders.

Workers in the area of juvenile justice need to be wary and critical of the often negative views associated with the families of offenders (Frost and Stein 1989). Simpson (1991), for example, provides an analysis of the way in which families are often pathologized in social inquiry reports. Yet, the exigencies of having to ensure compliance with court orders, of departmental requirements, and of heavy workloads may hinder processes of effective relationship building (Pitts 1990). The essentially disciplinary character of much juvenile justice intervention denotes a practice approach that is often determined by the requirements of the organization rather than the particular emotional and material needs of the clients.

For those social workers required to work directly with criminalized young people and their families, this study suggests that close attention needs to be paid to the micro-skills that are essential to establishing empowering relationships with families. A number of workers in this study, both police officers and social workers, were able to develop such a relationship within the disciplinary context. They were able to resist the tendency to categorize the families of juvenile offenders as dysfunctional, antisocial, or even criminogenic, a tendency that prevents the development of meaningful dialogue with parents and their children.

Besides skilled workers, it is obvious from this study that parents and families lack a framework of support when their children offend. The parents in this study suffered legal and welfare intervention that was concerned with juvenile crime and its reduction in fairly simplistic, quantitative terms. Parents' concerns are qualitative; they want to know how to understand and cope with what their children are doing. There may be any number of reasons why a supportive framework was generally not available to these parents; lack of staff, differing social priorities, or the low status of the parents of juvenile offenders may be some of the reasons. Comment on the UK Children Act 1989 by NACRO (1994: 4) sums it up well. Referring to the six key areas mentioned earlier, where parents could be supported and asked to play a greater role, the report states.

> There is however little evidence that systematic support work is taking place at local level to ensure that parents are playing a full and positive role in the key areas above. This is, in part, a question of resources and a question of competing priorities for local social services departments but it may also reflect a lack of guidance and how such specifically targeted work can be built into a more general framework of family support. There is a need to examine models of good practice and discuss how they might be implemented locally.

We do not claim that this study puts forward such a model of good practice; that was not our intention in doing this research. At the beginning of this book, we maintained that the valorization of the subject's voice, of personal narrative and experience, is essential in contesting the often spurious assumptions of many studies and in enabling those subject to disciplinary systems to voice their experiences in their own terms. What we offer those who wish to develop models of practice in juvenile justice are the voices of 20 families who have given some insight into the intimacy of family life when it is affected by the trauma of juvenile offending. While these narratives have limitations, they nonetheless offer an invaluable insight into the means by which the subjects of disciplinary systems articulate their experiences. Indeed, it is in the telling of personal stories that we begin to appreciate the importance of the meanings that families attach to their situations. These insights, we contend, provide a basis for developing the models of good practice that NACRO seeks.

REFERENCES

Abbott, P., and C. Wallace. 1992. *The Family and the New Right*. London: Pluto Press.

Alder, C., and J. Wundersitz. 1994. *Family Conferencing and Juvenile Justice*. Canberra, Australia: Australian Institute of Criminology.

Altatt, P., and J. Yeandle. 1992. *Youth Unemployment and the Family*. London: Routledge.

Anderson, M. 1994. What is New about the Modern Family? In *Time, Family and Community*. Edited by M. Drake. Milton Keynes: Open University Press.

Australian Association of Social Workers, 1995. 'Impounding Children Like Stray Dogs: The Children's (Parental Responsibility) Act.' *Social Policy Bulletin*, no. 4, June.

Australian Law Reform Commission. 1997. *Seen and Heard: Priorities for Children in the Legal Process*. Sydney: Australian Law Reform Commission.

Azevado, J. 1998. The Art of Tank Warfare: Think Tanks and Propaganda in the Australian Mass Media. Sunshine Coast University College, Queensland, Australia. Unpublished paper.

Bessant, J. 1996a. *Youth, Unemployment and Crime: Policy, Work and the 'Risk' Society.'* Melbourne, Victoria: Youth Research Centre.

Bessant, J. 1996b. The Discovery of an Australian Juvenile Underclass. *Australian and New Zealand Journal of Sociology* 31, no. 1: 32–48

Bessant, J., H. Sercombe, and R. Watts. 1998. *Youth Studies: An Australian Perspective*. Melbourne, Australia: Longman.

Blagg, H. 1997. A Just Measure of Shame: Aboriginal Youth and Conferencing in Australia. *British Journal of Criminology* 37, no. 4: 481–502.

Blagg, H., and D. Smith. 1989. *Crime, Penal Policy and Social Work*. London: Macmillan.
Bottoms, A. 1989. Neglected Features of Contemporary Penal Systems. In *The Power to Punish*. Edited by D. Garland and P. Young, London: Gower.
Bowlby, J. 1953. *Child Care and the Growth of Love*. Baltimore, MD: Penguin.
Braithwaite, J. 1989. *Crime, Shame and Reintegration*. Cambridge: Cambridge University Press.
Brake, M., and C. Hale. 1993. *Public Order and Private Lives*. London: Routledge and Kegan Paul.
Briggs, F. 1994. The Changing Family. In *Children and Families*. Edited by F. Briggs. St. Leonards, NSW: Allen and Unwin.
Campbell, A. 1987. Self Reported Delinquency and Home Life: Evidence from a Sample of British Girls. *Journal of Youth and Adolescence* 16, no. 2:
Campbell, B. 1994. *Goliath: Britain's Most Dangerous Places*. London: Macmillan.
Carrington, K. 1992. Policing Families and Controlling the Young. In *For Your Own Good*. Edited by R. White and B. Wilson. Bundoora, Victoria, Australia: La Trobe University Press.
Carrington, K. 1993. *Offending Girls: Sex, Youth and Justice*. Sydney: Allen and Unwin.
Cass, B. 1988. The Changing Nature of Dependence and the Concept of "Family Policy." In *Strategies for Australian Social Policy*. Edited by R. Henderson. Sydney: Allen and Unwin.
Centre for Independent Studies. 1997a. *Statistical Indicators of Australia's Well-Being*. Sydney: Centre for Independent Studies.
Centre for Independent Studies. 1997b. *Rising Crime in Australia*, Sydney: Centre for Independent Studies.
Chomsky, N. 1996. *Class Warfare: Interviews with David Barsamian*. Boston, MA: South End Press.
Cohen, S. 1974. Criminology and the Sociology of Deviance in Britain. In *Deviance and Social Control*. Edited by P. Rock and M. McIntosh. London: Tavistock.
Cohen, S. 1984. The Deeper Structures of the Law or "Beware of the Rulers Bearing Justice." *Contemporary Crisis* 8: 83–93.

Cohen, S. 1985. *Visions of Social Control: Crime, Punishment and Classification*, Cambridge, UK: Polity Press.

Cohen, S. 1994. Social Control and the Politics of Reconstruction. In *The Futures of Criminology*. Edited by D. Nelken, London: Sage.

Collins, C. 1990. *When Parents Pay for Their Children's Mistakes*, State Government News (California), June.

Connell, R. W., and T. H. Irving. 1992. *Class Structure in Australian History*. Melbourne, Australia: Longman Cheshire.

Consedine, R. 1995. *Restorative Justice: Healing the Effects of Crime*. Lyttleton, New Zealand: Ploughshares.

Cook, D. 1997. *Crime, Poverty and Disadvantage*. London: Child Poverty Action Group.

Davidson, H. 1996. No Consequences—Re-Examining Parental Responsibility Laws. *Stanford Law and Policy Review* 7, no. 1:

De Souza. 1994. Parents Against Crime: An Experimental Project. In *Families, Children and Crime*. Edited by A. Coote. London: Institute for Public Policy Research.

Denzin, N. K. 1989. *Interpretive Interactionism*. Newbury Park, CA: Sage.

DFYCC. 1998a. *Juvenile Justice Centres: A Discussion Paper*. Brisbane, Queensland: Department of Families, Youth and Community Care.

DFYCC. 1998b. *If Your Child Breaks the Law: A Parent's Guide*. Brisbane, Queensland: Department of Families, Youth and Community Care.

Devine, F. 1989. Privatised Families and Their Homes. In *Home and the Family: Creating the Domestic Sphere*. Edited by A. Garland and G. Crow. London: Macmillan.

Donaldson, M. 1991. *Time of Our Lives: Labour and Love in the Working Class.* Sydney: Allen and Unwin.

Donzelot, J. 1979. *The Policing of Families*. London: Heinemann.

Embling, J. 1986. *Fragmented Lives: A Darker Side of Australian Life*. Ringwood: Penguin.

Farrington, D. 1994. The Influence of the Family on Delinquent Development. In *Crime and the Family*. Edited by C. Henricson. London: Family Policy Studies Centre.

Feeley, M., and J. Simon. 1994. Actuarial Justice: The Emerging New Criminal Law. In *The Futures of Criminology*, ed. D. Nelken. London: Sage.

Finch, L. 1994. *The Classing Gaze*. Sydney: Allen and Unwin.

Finer, C. J., and M. Ellis, eds. 1998. *Crime and Social Exclusion*. Oxford: Blackwell.

Foucault, M. 1977. *Discipline and Punish: The Birth of the Prison*. Harmondsworth: Penguin.

Francis, J. 1993. Punitive Politics, Positive Practice. *Community Care* (December): 16–23.

Frost, N., and M. Stein. 1989. *The Politics of Child Welfare: Inequality, Power and Conflict*. London: Harvester-Wheatsheaf.

Garland, D. 1994. Of Crimes and Criminals: The Development of Criminology in Britain. In *The Oxford Handbook of Criminology*. Edited by M. Maguire, R. Morgan, and R. Reiner. Oxford: Clarendon.

Garland, D., and P. Young. 1983. Towards a Social Analysis of Penalty. In *The Power to Punish: Contemporary Penalty and Social Analysis*. Edited by D. Garland and P. Young. London: Heinemann.

Garland, D., and P. Young, eds. 1993. *The Power to Punish*. Aldershot: Gower.

Gilding, M. 1997. *Australian Families: An Australian Perspective*. Melbourne: Longman.

Gittins, D. 1993. *The Family in Question: Changing Households and Familiar Ideologies*. London: Macmillan.

Glueck, S., and E. Glueck. 1950. *Unravelling Juvenile Delinquency*. New York: Harper and Row.

Graham, J., and B. Bowling. 1996. *Young People and Crime*. London: Home Office Research Unit.

Hall, C. 1995. Silent and Silenced Voices: Interactional Construction of Audience in Social Work Talk. University of Bristol. Unpublished paper.

Halsbury's Statutes of England and Wales. 1992. Reissue (6). London: Butterworths.

Hartley, R., and I. Wolcott. 1994. *The Position of Young People in Relation to the Family*. Hobart: National Clearing House for Youth Studies.

Hil, R. 1994. Targeting and Control: Unmasking the Rhetoric of Queensland's Juvenile Crime Prevention Strategy *Transitions* 3, no. 3.

Hil, R. 1996. The Family Fix. *Arena Magazine* (June-July) no. 23: 35–38.

Hil, R. 1998. The Call to Order: Families, Responsibility and Juvenile Crime Control. *Journal of Australian Studies* 59, 101–114.

Hil, R., and A. McMahon. 1995. In the Shadows: the Silence and Silenced Family in Juvenile Justice Research. *Children Australia* 20, no. 4: 48.

Hil, R., A. McMahon, and A. Buckley. 1996. *Another Hole in the Wall: A progress report on a study of young people, crime and families in North Queensland*. Melbourne: Youth Research Centre, University of Melbourne.

Hill, D. 1994. Children of Change. *The Guardian*, December 29.

Hogg, R., and D. Brown. 1998. *Rethinking Law and Order*. Armadale: Pluto Press.

Holman, B. 1993. *A New Deal for Social Welfare*. Oxford: Lion Press.

Holman, B. 1995. *Children and Crime*. Oxford: Lion Press.

Home Office Research Unit. 1994. British Home Office Study.

Horwath, J., and A. Griggs. 1989. Parents Slipping Through the Loopholes. *Social Work Today*, October 19.

Hudson, B. 1987. *Justice Through Punishment*. London: Routledge and Kegan Paul.

Hudson, B. 1993. *Penal Policy and Social Justice*. London: Macmillan.

Hudson, B. 1996. *Understanding Justice: An Introduction to Ideas, Perspectives and Controversies in Modern Penal Theory*. Buckingham: Open University Press.

Jamrozik, A., and Sweeney, T. 1996. *Children and Society: The Family, the State and Social Parenthood*. Melbourne: Macmillan.

Jeffs, T., and M. Smith. 1990. Demography, Location and Young People. In *Young People, Inequality and Youth Crime*. Edited by T. Jeffs and M. Smith, London: Macmillan.

Ife, J. 1997. *Rethinking Social Work: Towards Critical Practice*. Melbourne: Longman.

Junger-Tass, J. 1994. The Changing Family and its Relationship with Delinquent Behaviour. In *Crime and the Family*. Edited by L. Henricson. London: Family Policy Studies Centre, 1994.

Knapp, M. S. 1995. How Shall We Study Comprehensive, Collaborative Services for Children and Families. *Educational Researcher* 24: 5–16.

Laub, J., and R. Sampson. 1988. Unraveling Families and Delinquency: A re-analysis of the Gluecks Data. *Criminology* 26, no 3: 355–79.

Lee, R. M., and C. M. Renzetti. 1993. The Problems of Researching Sensitive Topics: An Overview and Introduction. In *Researching Sensitive Topics*. Edited by C. M. Renzetti and R. M. Lee, 313. Newbury Park: Sage.

Leflore, L. 1988. Delinquent Youths and Family. *Adolescence* 23, no. 91: 629–42.

Lincoln Y. S., and E. G. Guba. 1985. *Naturalistic Inquiry*. Beverly Hills, CA: Sage.

Lindsay, P. 1996. Press release, Federal Liberal Party (Townsville, Queensland), April 23.

Lister, R. 1996. Back to the Family: Family Policies and Politics Under the Major Government. In *The Politics of the Family*. Edited by H. Jones and J. Miller. Avebury: Aldershot.

Lowry, G. 1994. The Family as a Context for Delinquency Prevention. In *Families, Schools and Delinquency Prevention*. Edited by J. Q. Wilson and G. Lowry. New York: Springer.

Maguire, F. 1995. *Children's Court of Queensland: Third Annual Report*. Brisbane: Children's Court.

Maxwell, M., and A. Morris. 1993. *Families, Victims and Culture: Youth Justice in New Zealand*. Wellington: Institute of Criminology, Victoria University of Wellington.

McMahon, A. 1997. Rough Justice: Juveniles and the Reporting of Crime in Townsville. In *Youth, Crime and the Media*. Edited by J. Bessant and R. Hil. Hobart: National Clearinghouse for Youth Studies.

Meredith, R. 1996. Parents Convicted for a Youth's Misconduct. *New York Times*, October 5.

Minichiello, V., R. Aroni, E. Timewell, and L. Alexander. 1990. *In-Depth Interviewing: Researching People*. Melbourne: Longman Cheshire.

Morgan, P. 1978. *Delinquent Fantasies*. London: Temple Smith.

Morrison, B. 1998. *As If*. London: Granta Books.

NACRO. 1994. *Young Offenders Committee, Policy Paper 4: Partnership with Parents in Dealing with Young Offenders.* London: National Association for the Care and Resettlement of Offenders.
Naffine, N. 1993. Philosophies of Juvenile Justice. In *Juvenile Justice: Debating the Issues.* Edited by F. Gale, N. Naffine, and J. Wundersitz. Sydney: Allen and Unwin.
Naffine, N. 1997. *Feminism and Criminolgy.* Oxford: Polity Press.
National Council for the International Year of the Family. 1994. *Creating the Links: Families and Social Responsibility.* Canberra: Australian Government Publishing Service.
Nichols, H. 1985. Children's Aid Panels in South Australia. In *Juvenile Delinquency in Australia.* Edited by A. Borowski and J. M. Murray. Melbourne: Methuen.
O'Connor, I. 1992. *Youth, Crime and Justice in Queensland.* Brisbane: Criminal Justice Commission.
O'Malley, P. 1996. Post-Social Criminologies: Some Implications of Current Political Trends for Criminology Theory and Practice. *Current Issues in Criminal Justice* 8, no. 1: 26–38
Parton, N. 1991. *Governing the Family: Childcare, Child Protection and the State.* London: Macmillan.
Penal Affairs Consortium. 1994. *Parents and Juvenile Crime*, London: PAC.
Pilger, J. 1998. *Hidden Agendas.* London: Vintage Books.
Pinkney, S. 1994. Fights Over Family: Competing Discourses in the Two Decades Before the International Year of the Family. *Just Policy* no.2 (March):
Pitts, J. 1990. *Working with Young Offenders.* London: Macmillan.
Pitts, J. 1998. *The New Politics of Juvenile Justice.* London: Macmillan.
Polk, K. 1994. Family Conferencing: Theoretical and Evaluative Questions. In *Family Conferencing and Juvenile Justice.* Edited by C. Alder and J. Wundersitz. Canberra: Australian Institute of Criminology.
Pratt, J. 1993. Welfare and Justice: Incompatable Philosophies. In *Juvenile Justice: Debating the Issues.* Edited by F. Gale, N. Naffine and J. Wundersitz. Sydney: Allen and Unwin.
Radford, N. 1992. Strengthening Family Units and Helping Parents to Be Responsible and Accountable. Paper presented to the

Australian Institute of Criminology National Conference on Juvenile Crime, September 22–24, Adelaide, S. A.

Rankin, J. H. 1983. The Family Context of Delinquency. *Social Problems* 30, no. 4: 466–79.

Rigoli, R. M., and J. Hewitt. 1991. *Delinquency and Society: A Child-Centred Approach.* New York: McGraw Hill.

Richards, L. 1990. *Nobody's Home: Dreams and Realities in the New Suburbia.* Melbourne: Oxford University Press.

Roach-Anleu, S. 1991. *Deviance, Conformity and Social Control.* Melbourne: Longman.

Rose, D. 1994. *In the Name of the Law: The Collapse of Criminal Justice.* London: Vintage.

Rose, N. 1990. *Governing the Soul: The Shaping of the Private Self.* London: Routledge.

Rutter, M. 1972. *Maternal Deprivation Reassessed.* Harmondsworth: Penguin.

Rutter, M., and H. Giller. 1983. *Juvenile Delinquency: Trends and Perspectives.* Harmondsworth: Penguin.

Sandor, D. 1994. The 'Thickening Blue Wedge in Juvenile Justice'. In *Family Conferencing and Juvenile Justice.* Edited by C. Alder, and J. Wundersitz. Canberra: Australian Institute of Criminology.

Sarantakos, S. 1996. *Modern Families: An Australian Perspective.* Melbourne: Macmillan.

Simpson, B., and C. Simpson. 1993. The Use of Curfews to Control Juvenile Offending in Australia: Managing Crime or Wasting Time? *Current Issues in Criminal Justice* 5, no. 2: 184–99.

Simpson, C. 1991. Increasing Family Responsibility and Juvenile Justice. Master's thesis. La Trobe University, Department of Legal Studies, Bundoora.

Smith, D. 1996. *Criminology and Social Work.* London: Macmillan.

Straw, J., and S. Anderson. 1996. *Parenting: A Discussion Paper.* London: New Labor Headquarters.

Thomas, K., and H. Heim. 1993a. *Youth Study Self Report Survey—Cairns.* Brisbane: Community Development and Crime Prevention Unit, Justice Studies, Queensland University of Technology.

Thomas, K., and H. Heim. 1993b. *Results of a Self Report Youth Survey in Mackay City and the Pioneer Shire*. Brisbane: Community Development and Crime Prevention Unit, Justice Studies, Queensland University of Technology.

Thomas, K., H. Heim, and T. O'Connor. 1993. *Family Factors in Youth Offending: Implications for the Reorganisation of Voluntary Work in Community Crime Prevention*. Brisbane: Justice Studies, Faculty of Law, Queensland University of Technology.

Toughlove International 1998. History of Toughlove. URL: http://www.toughlove.org/history.htm (accessed December 6, 1998).

Tygart, C. E. 1991. Juvenile Delinquency and Number of Children in a Family. *Youth and Society* 22, no 2: 525–536.

Utting, D. 1994. Family Factors and the Rise in Crime. In *Families, Children and Crime*. Edited by A. Coote. London: Institute of Public Policy Research.

Utting, D. 1995. When the Talking Has to Stop. *The Guardian*, February 22.

Utting, D., J. Bright, and C. Henricson. 1994. *Crime and the Family: Improving Child Rearing and Preventing Delinquency*. London: Family Policy Studies Centre.

Von Hirsh, A. 1976. *Doing Justice: The Choice of Punishments*. New York: Hill and Wang.

Von Hirsh, A. 1993. *Censure and Sanctions*, Oxford: Clarendon Press.

Weeks, W., and J. Wilson. 1993. *Issues Facing Australian Families: Human Services Respond*. Melbourne: Longman Cheshire.

Wells, L. E., and J. H. Rankin. 1986. The Broken Homes Model of Delinquency: Analytical Issues. *Journal of Researching Crime and Delinquency* 23, no. 1:

West, D. J. 1982. *Delinquency: Its Roots, Causes and Prospects*. Cambridge: Harvard University Press.

White, R. 1994. Shaming and Reintegrative Strategies: Individuals, State Power and Social Interest. In *Family Conferencing and Juvenile Justice*. Edited by C. Alder and J. Wundersitz. Canberra, Australia: Australian Institute of Criminology.

Wilson, J. Q., and R. J. Herrnstein. 1985. *Crime and Human Nature*. New York: Basic Books.

Winnicott, D. 1964. *The Child, the Family and the Outside World*. Harmondsworth: Penguin.
Winnicott, D. 1968. *The Family and Individual Development*. London: Tavistock.
Winnicott, D. 1984. *Deprivation and Delinquency*. London: Tavistock.
Yea, A. 1997. Holding Parents Responsible, *NCLS Legislator* 5, no. 7.
Young, A. 1996. *Imagining Crime: Textual Outlaws and Criminal Conversations*. London: Sage.
Youth Justice Coalition. 1990. *Kids in Justice: A Blueprint for the 90s*. Sydney: YJC.

INDEX

Ailing state of the family 18

'Back to basics' campaign 23
best-practice parenting 25
blame, significant factor 107
blaming parents 124

Child Crime Teams 161
   early intervention 161
children, offending 8, 9
Children's Court 131, 149
   sentencing 152-3
community panels 38
community conferencing 35, 36, 38
control
   community 27-43
   parental 2, 117
crime
   alleged causes 24
   control 28
   juvenile 15
   waves 4
criminal justice 28
criminogenic tendency 3, 48, 59
cultural norms 15, 20
curfews 41

Delinquency 2-3, 18, 45-63
dysfunctional family 49

'Epidemics' of offending 15
   government action 15
explanations
   offending behavior 107
   offending theories 120
external factors 119

Families and crime
   psychological theories 45
families and juvenile crime 16-26
   community control 31
   disadvantaged 17
   explanations for offending behavior 107-129
   middleclass 17
   poor 17
   powerlessness 39
   restitution proceedings 163-171
family
   ailing 18
   blaming 107
   breakdown 17, 24
   broken 51
   functioning 48
   internal dynamics 54, 57, 117
   pathological 49-51
   relationship 60
   responsibility 174

structure 52, 58
traditional 16

Indigenous Australians 5, 6, 139
  cultural knowledge and skills 144
  Departmental guidelines 148
  perspectives 127
  'race', crucial subtext 6
  worker, Family Services 144

Juvenile
  control 25
  delinquency 46
  offending, causes 129
  parents' experiences 28
Juvenile Justice 135
  service providers 139

Lawlessness 1, 15
legislation 157–161
localized approaches 11

Maternal deprivation 24, 51, 107
material conditions 61
media 24, 125, 156
moral authority 23
moral frameworks 22
moral guidance 23
moral panic 15
mother(s) 21, 63
multivariate factors 113

New Right 18, 19, 22

Offenders' theories 120
offending behaviors 19
  explanations 107
  external pressures 108

family functioning 108
  psychological reasons 108
organizational perspective 12

Parent(s)
  blaming 16, 124
  capacity to care 33
  child relations 53
  culpability, media emphasis 107;
  feminist critics 48
  media scapegoat 129
  (and the) police 131
  single 16, 20
  training in skills 54
parental restitution 155–179
  culpable action 159
  penalizing the parents 160
  supervision 53
police, parents and the 131
political discourse 16
positivistic approach 58
predictive indicators 55, 61
professional responses 179
punitive individualism 155

Quality of care 49

Race, crucial subtext 6
research and research subjects
  complexities 9–10
  positivist 58
  voices of those researched 83
restitution 155–171
restorative justice 26

Social control 127
social disorder and the family 18, 160
socioeconomic factors 49
social values 16

State agencies   129
systems of juvenile crime control
    11

Teen gangs   15
theories, offenders'   120
theory
    critical social   3
    criminological   30
    individualistic   47
    rational choice   30
Tough Love   115
traditional values   11
traditional structures   23

Underclass, characteristics   23
unemployment   23

Violence, emergence   18

Welfare dependency   23
welfarism   29, 39

General Editors: Joseph & Linda DeVitis

As schools struggle to redefine and restructure themselves, they need to be cognizant of the new realities of adolescents. Thus, this series of monographs and textbooks is committed to depicting the variety of adolescent cultures that exist in today's post-industrial societies. It is intended to be a primarily qualitative research, practice, and policy series devoted to contextual interpretation and analysis that encompasses a broad range of interdisciplinary critique. In addition, this series will seek to provide a pragmatic, pro-active response to the current backlash of conservatism that continues to dominate political discourse, practice, and policy. This series seeks to address issues of curriculum theory and practice; multicultural education; aggression and violence; the media and arts; school dropouts; homeless and runaway youth; alienated youth; at-risk adolescent populations; family structures and parental involvement; and race, ethnicity, class, and gender studies.

Send proposals and manuscripts to the General Editors at:
> Joseph & Linda DeVitis
> Binghamton University
> Dept. of Education & Human Development
> Binghamton, NY 13902

To order other books in this series, please contact our Customer Service Department at:
> (800) 770-LANG (within the U.S.)
> (212) 647-7706 (outside the U.S.)
> (212) 647-7707 FAX

or browse online by series at:
> WWW.PETERLANGUSA.COM